Representing the Advantaged

Political inequality is a major issue in American politics, with racial minorities and low-income voters receiving less favorable representation. Scholars argue that this political inequality stems largely from differences in political participation and that if all citizens participated equally we would achieve political equality. Daniel M. Butler shows that this common view is incorrect. He uses innovative field and survey experiments involving public officials to show that a significant amount of bias in representation traces its roots to the information, opinions, and attitudes that politicians bring to office and suggests that even if all voters participated equally, there would still be significant levels of bias in American politics. Butler's work provides a new theoretical basis for understanding inequality in American politics and insights into what institutional changes can be used to fix the problem.

Daniel M. Butler is an associate professor of political science at Washington University in St. Louis. His work has been published in such journals as the *American Journal of Political Science*, the *Journal of Politics, Legislative Studies Quarterly, Political Analysis*, and the *Quarterly Journal of Political Science*. Butler is a cofounder and co-organizer of the Symposium on the Politics of Immigration, Race, and Ethnicity (SPIRE), a regular meeting of scholars doing research in race and ethnic politics in the United States, and the founder and director of the Laboratories of Democracy (labsofdemocracy.org), a network of academics who collaborate with nonprofits and public officials to design and conduct randomized experiments aimed at maximizing policy effectiveness. He earned a PhD in political science from Stanford University, where his research was supported by a graduate research fellowship from the National Science Foundation.

Representing the Advantaged

How Politicians Reinforce Inequality

DANIEL M. BUTLER
Washington University in St. Louis

CAMBRIDGE
UNIVERSITY PRESS

CAMBRIDGE
UNIVERSITY PRESS

32 Avenue of the Americas, New York NY 10013-2473, USA

Cambridge University Press is part of the University of Cambridge.

It furthers the University's mission by disseminating knowledge in the pursuit of education, learning and research at the highest international levels of excellence.

www.cambridge.org
Information on this title: www.cambridge.org/9781107428720

© Daniel M. Butler 2014

First published 2014

A catalogue record for this publication is available from the British Library

Library of Congress Cataloguing in Publication data
Butler, Daniel M., 1980–
Representing the advantaged : how politicians reinforce inequality / Daniel M. Butler.
    pages   cm
Includes bibliographical references and index.
ISBN 978-1-107-07572-6 (hardback) – ISBN 978-1-107-42872-0 (paperback)
1. Political participation – United States.   2. Minorities – Political activity – United States.
3. Poor – Political activity – United States.   4. Proportional representation – United States.
5. Representative government and representation – United States.   I. Title.
JK1764.B89   2014
323.5–dc23   2014007193

ISBN 978-1-107-07572-6 Hardback
ISBN 978-1-107-42872-0 Paperback

Contents

Acknowledgments

I first wish to thank the Institution of Social and Policy Studies at Yale University and its directors – Don Green and Jacob Hacker – for funding this research and providing generous feedback. Thank you Don and Jacob!

I also must thank the amazing collaborators I have worked with over the years. I have been fortunate to work with smart, hardworking people. Two of these colleagues deserve special notice because our collaborative work has found its way into this manuscript. First, I want to thank Shang E. Ha for his collaboration in designing the two mayoral experiments found in Chapter 5. Second, I want to thank David Broockman for his work on our original article, which appeared in the *American Journal of Political Science*. David was a full collaborator in designing, implementing, and writing up the study. While these excellent scholars were full collaborators, they bear no responsibility for how I have interpreted the results of those studies herein.

I also want to acknowledge the *American Journal of Political Science* and the Midwest Political Science Association for allowing me to publish some of the original work that appeared there in my 2011 article with David Broockman "Do Politicians Racially Discriminate against Constituents? A Field Experiment on State Legislators." Material from that work serves as part of the material presented in Chapter 6.

I also wish to thank the following for providing feedback on early drafts of this work: Quintin Beazer, David Broockman, John Bullock, Richard Butler, Jason Casellas, Samuel DeCanio, Ryan Enos, Morris Fiorina, Don Green, Jacob Hacker, Zoltan Hajnal, Eitan Hersh, Seth Hill, Greg Huber, Jennifer Lawless, Matt Levendusky, David Mayhew, Jacob Montgomery, David Nickerson,

Eleanor Powell, Ken Scheve, Brian Slattery, Ali Valenzuela, Jim Vreeland, and Sophia Wallace. Their comments and the feedback from the anonymous reviewers made the project significantly better.

Finally, I wish to thank my family for giving me the support to accomplish all that I do. Thank you Deb!

Representatives as the Source of Bias

In 2004 the American Political Science Association's task force on inequality and American democracy released a report highlighting how the United States was failing to provide political equality in representation. This report is alarming because equality in representation – the degree to which politicians act evenhandedly in pursuing each citizen's preferences and interests – is a standard that is widely used to measure a democracy's health. Citing a variety of academic studies, the report noted the tendency of the U.S. government to systematically enact the policies preferred by the wealthy.

The members of the task force blamed the existing inequality on differences in political activity.

Citizens with lower and moderate incomes speak with a whisper that is lost on the ears of inattentive government officials, while the advantaged roar with a clarity and consistency that policy-makers readily hear and routinely follow. (APSA Task Force 2004, 1)

The task force went on to suggest that increasing all citizens' various forms of political participation would be the most effective way to end inequality. In this sense, the APSA task force report joins the bulk of political science research, which assumes that bias in participation is the source of bias in representation. Scholars argue that if all citizens exhibited similar levels of political activity we would achieve equality in representation.

While commonplace, this view is wrong. Equality in participation does not guarantee equality in representation. In this book I argue and present evidence showing that even if all voters participate (and donate money, contact their representatives, etc.) at equal rates, we will still observe bias in representation.

Bias in representation, at least in part, traces its roots to the people who are elected to office. We have underestimated the importance of this bias because our dominant paradigm of representation implicitly assumes that politicians are blank slates when they come to office. Politicians are not blank slates, and the information, opinions, and attitudes that they bring to office lead to significant bias in representation.

Further, politicians' backgrounds can lead to bias in representation in two different ways. First, their personal preferences lead them to exhibit bias in favor of some constituents. Second, their background makes it less costly to work on issues that are important to people like them. Because reelection-motivated politicians are interested in winning the most votes with the least amount of resources, the information they bring to office will, ceteris paribus, cause elected officials to work more on the issues important to people like them. As a result, politicians will as a whole give less attention to the issues that are important to the groups that are numerically underrepresented in office.

Evidence of Bias in Representation

Understanding the source of bias in representation is important because a growing literature documents the severe degree of political inequality. For example, on issues that are important to high-income earners (taxes, government spending, and Social Security), President Reagan's public positions were much closer to the preferences of high-income Americans than to those of low-income Americans as measured by Reagan's own internal polling data. In fact, when controlling for the opinions of high-income earners on these issues, the preferences of ideological conservatives no longer predict President Reagan's positions (Druckman and Jacobs 2011). Similarly, for the issues on which the wealthy disagree with either poor or middle-income individuals, the preferences of the wealthy strongly predict policy change while the preferences of their poor counterparts are uncorrelated with policy change (Gilens 2005, 2009, 2012). The same pattern holds even when you look at legislators' overall ideology; the preferences of the low-income constituents do not predict legislators' positions after controlling for the preferences of middle-income and wealthier citizens (Bartels 2008; see also Jacobs and Page 2005; Rigby and Wright 2011; Ellis 2012; cf. Ura and Ellis 2008; Stimson 2009; Wlezien and Soroka 2011). The views of the wealthy, whatever those views might be, tend to prevail.

Scholars have also raised concerns that racial minorities' interests are similarly underrepresented. Recent studies, for example, document how the gap between legislators' voting records and the ideological preferences of their constituents is larger for Latinos and blacks than for non-Latino white constituents (Griffin and Newman 2007, 2008). Further, the numerical underrepresentation of minorities in office leads to numerous ways in which minority constituents are disadvantaged relative to their white counterparts (see also

Cameron, Epstein, and O'Halloran 1996; Lublin 1997; Whitby 1997; Haynie 2001; Tate 2003; Wallace 2010; Minta 2009, 2011).

Could This Bias Simply Arise from Differences in Turnout?

The conventional view within political science is that this political inequality stems purely (or at least predominantly) from differences in who votes, donates money, and otherwise politically participates (e.g., Verba and Nie 1972; Piven and Cloward 1988; Rosenstone and Hansen 1993; Verba, Schlozman, and Brady 1995; Lijphart 1997; APSA Task Force 2004; Schlozman, Verba, and Brady 2012). The reason for implicating differences in political participation is, as Sidney Verba puts it, that "equal activity is crucial for equal consideration since political activity is the means by which citizens make their needs and preferences known to governing elites and induce them to be responsive" (2003: 663). However, even when constituents send the same message, their messages might not be given equal weight.

Indeed, the most extensive studies on inequality and representation cast doubt on this solution. Bartels (2008), for example, explores whether differences in participation or knowledge might explain the favoritism that wealthier constituents enjoy. He analyzes this question by weighting constituents' opinions by the differences in their levels of knowledge and political participation. He concludes that "allowing for differences in turnout, knowledge, and contacting reduces only modestly the substantial income-based disparities in responsiveness" (p. 279). Similarly, Griffin and Newman find that "voters are better represented than non-voters, but that this mainly applies to whites" (2008: 194). I add to this evidence by conducting experiments that show that bias in representation exists even when groups ask the same question and exhibit the same level of effort.

If differences in participation alone cannot explain bias in representation, what does?

The Missing Piece of the Puzzle: Politicians' Backgrounds

Bias arises because politicians are not adaptable blank slates when they come to office. The information, opinions, and attitudes that they bring to office lead to significant bias in representation.

Politicians' Personal Preferences as a Source of Bias

One way in which politicians are not blank slates is that they have personal preferences that lead to bias. Put simply, elected officials do not exhibit neutrality. They come to office with attitudes and preferences and may be willing to lose votes in order to exhibit bias in favor of their preferred constituents.

While I am not the first to observe that politicians' personal backgrounds affect representation, I make two important contributions.[1]

First, I design experiments that control for the nature of constituents' requests and the efforts they put into those requests (i.e., the demand side of representation). As noted in the earlier discussion, much of the research has focused on differences in constituents' participation to explain inequality. I design experiments in which the putative constituents are all using the same language to make the same requests. While holding constant the requests that are made, the experiments vary some aspect of the person asking for help (either race, gender, or socioeconomic status [SES]). For example, Chapter 6 presents the results from an experiment in which legislators are asked for help in navigating some aspect of the government bureaucracy (e.g., registering to vote). The results of the experiment show that legislators from both parties are more likely to respond to these requests for help when they come from a constituent from their own racial group: white legislators are more responsive to white constituents and minority legislators to minority constituents. This pattern emerges even though the constituents are asking for the same type of help. In other words, politicians exhibit significant bias even after controlling for demand-side considerations.

Second, I test whether politicians' bias affects racial minorities, women, and low-income constituents in different ways. In Chapter 4, for example, I look at whether politicians exhibit a bias against any of these groups when they evaluate constituents' opinions. I look at bias in the way politicians evaluate constituents' opinions because this is a key part of the input stage of the process, when politicians gather information about voters' preferences. In Chapter 6, I then look at whether they exhibit a bias against any of these groups when they decide whether to help constituents. These studies allow me to examine the role of bias directly at the output stage of the process, when politicians are deciding

---

[1] Burden (2007), for example, argues in favor of the "personal roots of representation," showing that tobacco use, religious affiliation, and choices with regard to using public schools all predict legislators' behavior in office. Legislators' demographics also strongly predict their behavior. Women vote differently on gender-related issues such as abortion and women's health (Tatalovitch and Schier 1993; Burrell 1994; Dolan 1997; Swers 1998), and legislators from working-class backgrounds are more liberal and more likely to support issues important to organized labor in their roll call votes (Carnes 2012). Cameron, Epstein, and O'Halloran (1996) found that black legislators are more likely to support civil rights issues (for voting differences between blacks and whites, see also Whitby 1997; Lublin 1997), which may be explained by blacks' sense of linked fate (Dawson 1994). Descriptive representation (see Pitkin 1967; Reingold 2008) also affects the bills that legislators sponsor (Bratton and Haynie 1999; Haynie 2001; Sinclair-Chapman 2002; Swers 2002; Wolbrecht 2002; Bratton 2005; Orey et al. 2006; Burden 2007; Gerrity, Osborn, and Mendez 2007; Rocca, Sanchez, and Uscinski 2008), how much they participate in committee activities of interest to voters (Gamble 2007; Minta 2009, 2011), how they perform constituency service (Canon 1999; Grose 2011), the symbolic benefits that constituents receive (Tate 2003; Sinclair-Chapman and Price 2008), and the types of federal spending they bring to the district (Grose 2011).

what actions to take. I find that politicians exhibit a direct bias against racial minorities when deciding to help them with simple requests and a bias against low-SES voters when evaluating their opinions, but not vice versa. Politicians do not exhibit either of these biases against women.[2]

Showing that different groups face different biases provides insights into what can be done to help underrepresented groups. If we understand when bias occurs, we can design political institutions that mitigate that bias. In the conclusion I discuss some potential institutional fixes to help politically disadvantaged groups in light of my results.

Differences in Information as a Source of Bias

Another way in which politicians are not blank slates is that they come to office with information based on their personal experiences, which makes it more efficient for reelection-seeking politicians to focus on issues that are important to people like them. Empirical studies of representation have not considered the possibility that differences in information can be an important source of bias in representation. Yet this is an important way in which legislators' backgrounds can influence inequality and is theoretically quite distinct from the effect of politicians' personal preferences. For example, the arguments about politicians' personal preferences assume that they are willing to lose votes in order to exhibit favoritism toward their preferred constituents. In contrast, the information and efficiency argument suggests that bias arises *because they are trying to win votes*. In particular, strategic, reelection-motivated politicians will focus on winning the most votes they can while expending the least amount of resources.

An important way in which politicians win votes is by working on issues important to donors and voters (Fenno 1973). Because working on issues takes time and effort, the strategic politician will be more likely to work on issues about which he or she has personal knowledge and information. It is simply more efficient for politicians to expend their efforts in the areas about which they are most knowledgeable.

Legislators' own backgrounds are an important source of this type of information. Those who choose to send their children to private schools, for example, are likely to know more about the private school system (Burden 2007). Women, on both sides of the issue, may have thought more about issues related to abortion and women's health (Swers 2002).

The information that legislators bring to office can in turn shape how they spend their time and resources. Politicians from a wealthier business

---

[2] These patterns suggest that at least one important source of the bias that legislators exhibit comes from their social interactions. As Americans we live in neighborhoods that are divided along racial and economic lines. We also are more likely to interact socially with people who share our racial and economic background. In contrast, our social experiences are not so sharply divided along gender lines (McPherson, Smith-Lovin, and Cook 2001).

background may spend more time helping constituents and working on issues related to setting up a business because they have more experience in that area. By contrast, a politician from a poorer, working-class background may understand more about what it is like to navigate government programs so as to receive welfare benefits and so may spend more time on that issue. Politicians' personal information incentivizes them to focus on issues that are more important to people who share their backgrounds because it is easier for them to do so.

The results from Chapter 5 show that a politician's drive for efficiency can lead to bias that favors the interests of constituents who share some aspect of his or her background. In one of the experiments, city officials receive a request to learn more about programs at their local high school. Some of the officials are asked about the availability of advanced placement courses while others are asked whether there is a free lunch program. Consistent with the possibility that wealthier mayors are less likely to have personal knowledge about free lunch programs, we find that mayors from wealthier cities are significantly less likely to answer questions related to free lunch programs (and at the same time very likely to answer questions related to their local high school's advanced placement program).

Significantly, the bias in politicians' proactive actions is not driven by animus or even overt favoritism for one's own group. This bias will occur even if politicians do not have any personal biases. Rather, the bias occurs because strategic politicians who are trying to get reelected play to their strengths.

The aggregate consequence of this efficiency-driven behavior is that groups that are numerically underrepresented in office are at a disadvantage. The issues that these groups care about will not receive the time and attention that other issues receive.

Bias in representation cannot be understood simply by looking at differences in participation because bias traces its roots to the people who are elected to office. We can only fully understand bias in representation if we realize that politicians are not blank slates when they come to office. The information, opinions, and attitudes that politicians bring to office lead to the biases we observe. I design a series of experiments to test this argument.

The Experimental Advantage

I contribute to the existing literature on political inequality by conducting experiments that increase our confidence in the empirical regularities I uncover. A major reason that previous studies have not done more to understand when representation breaks down is that previous scholars have raised doubts that bias in representation exists at all (e.g., Swain 1993; Ura and Ellis 2008; Wlezien and Soroka 2011). If there are no inequalities in representation, there is no need to study the question in more depth. Providing convincing evidence that there is inequality in representation is difficult, and so it is understandable that previous research has focused on trying to establish more confidence in the basic empirical relationship. My experimental research design provides this confidence in understanding potential breakdowns in the representation process.

I make another novel contribution to the study of representation and inequality by using experiments in which *political elites* are the subjects under study. While studies using lab participants – most often university undergraduates – or regular citizens yield valuable insights into voter behavior, there are reasons to doubt that these results apply to elected officials (Sears 1986; Butler and Kousser 2013). My research offers new insights by directly studying the behavior of elected officials.

The experimental approach helps me solve problems that have stymied the potential impact of previous research. Chapter 6, for example, presents experiments on legislators' casework behavior to understand the role of race in determining how officials serve their constituents. A few previous studies on descriptive representation have also considered legislators' casework behavior. Canon (1999) looks at the racial background of staff hired to work in Washington, DC, offices and the racial content of newsletters. Grose (2011) looks at the racial composition of the neighborhoods where legislators locate their district offices and the racial backgrounds of legislative staff members who work in those offices (see also Swain 1993). These studies are important, but they cannot tell us whether the outcomes for constituents are different because white and minority legislators treat minority constituents differently. Black legislators are more likely to locate their offices in black neighborhoods, but this may be driven in part by increased demand from black constituents for help when they are served by a black representative. Indeed, staffers from Harold Ford Jr.'s office reported that black constituents disproportionately sought help from Congressman Ford (Grose 2011, 128).[3] We can only test whether descriptive representation influences the supply side of casework service when the constituents' requests are held constant.

I hold the demand side constant by conducting constituency service field experiments in which legislators are sent similar requests. I vary the race and ethnicity of the putative constituents sending the requests to see whether

---

[3] This concern is not limited to questions of inequality and race. Sidney Verba (2003) provides an overview of the literature on inequality in politics and notes that while the focus has been on understanding differences in who votes, donates money, and otherwise politically participates (e.g., Verba and Nie 1972; Piven and Cloward 1988; Rosenstone and Hansen 1993; Verba, Schlozman, and Brady 1995; Lijphart 1997), we still do not know much about whether groups are treated equally when they communicate with or seek access to public institutions. Verba notes, "The literature on the receipt of messages and the response to them is not as well developed as that on the messages sent" (2003, 666). My constituency service field experiments allow me to see whether race/ethnicity, gender, and socioeconomic status influence how responsive legislators are when constituents contact them.

legislators are more responsive to requests from constituents from the same racial or ethnic group as themselves.

Existing studies have also been unable to differentiate between the effect of information and other factors, such as preferences, on politicians' behavior. For example, previous studies have found that female legislators in Congress participate more in floor debates on women's issues (Tamerius 1995; Swers 2001) and advocate for women's interests to be incorporated into committee legislation (Dodson 1998, 2006; Swers 2002). Female legislators may do this because they have more knowledge and information about these issues. It is also possible, however, that they simply prioritize these issues more (Thomas and Welch 1991; Reingold 1992; Thomas 1994, 1997; Foerstel and Foerstel 1996).

I isolate the potential differences in knowledge and information by conducting three constituency service field experiments. Again, these experiments involve contacting public officials with a simple request. However, instead of varying the descriptive characteristics of the individual contacting the elected official, I hold those descriptive characteristics constant and see whether varying the message's content affects the level of responsiveness. These experiments allow me to see whether elected officials are more likely to answer questions on topics they are more likely to have personal experience with.

The substantive payoff of these experiments is that they allow me to rule out the possibility that inequality in representation is purely the result of differences in participation. Even when the same requests are made with the same level of effort, some groups face a distinct disadvantage. That is not to say that participation is not important. Rather, the point is that significant bias would exist even if there were no differences in political participation. In other words, even if the rich did not make more political donations and enjoy greater political access, they would still enjoy better political representation. Bias would remain because bias begins with who is elected to office. The information and preferences that politicians bring to office lead them to favor some constituents over others.

Outline of the Rest of the Book

The remainder of this book follows a straightforward outline. Chapter 2 discusses how representation can break down. In Chapter 3, I comment generally on the constituency service field experiments that I conduct. Chapters 4, 5, and 6 present experimental tests of the different forms of bias I outline in Chapter 2. Chapter 7 provides a discussion of the political and policy implications of the results.

Chapter 2

In Chapter 2, I discuss how acknowledging that politicians are not fully adaptable actors who come to office as blank slates can explain why, at some point between constituents having preferences on an issue and elected officials taking actions on that issue, bias moves the outcome away from the preferences of low-income and racial minorities. Determining where the breakdown occurs depends on understanding the different stages of the representation process. In this chapter, I discuss three stages of that process: (a) when elected officials process constituents' opinions, (b) when they decide what issues to work on, and (c) when they use the inputs they have to create legislative outputs. In later chapters I test for bias in these different parts of the process.

Chapter 3
Chapter 3 discusses the issues in designing and interpreting constituency service field experiments. I devote a chapter to discussing these issues because constituency service experiments are powerful tools that have not been widely used in political science.

I also present a pair of constituency service experiments that examine whether retiring legislators become less responsive to requests for help to see if there is evidence that legislators view this type of service as a duty (Fiorina 1989). I find strong evidence that they act as if this type of service is one of their legislative duties.

Chapter 4
In Chapter 4, I use a series of survey experiments to test whether elected officials systematically discount the opinions of some groups when they learn about constituents' preferences. The experiments show that public officials discount the intensity and thoughtfulness of low-income constituents' opinions. They do not exhibit any gender or racial bias in the way they process constituents' opinions. Interestingly, the benefits of descriptive representation do not appear to mitigate the bias against low-SES constituents. If anything, low-income officials exhibit a greater bias in favor of high-SES constituents than their high-income counterparts do.

Chapter 5
In Chapter 5, I present three constituency service field experiments, which show that public officials' personal background, experience, and knowledge make them more prepared to take proactive actions on policy issues related to their background. In testing the role of gender, I find that male legislators are less responsive to questions dealing with women's issues than they are to questions dealing with other issues, while female legislators are equally responsive to questions dealing with women's issues and questions dealing with other issues. Similarly, Shang Ha and I find evidence that city mayors are more likely to answer questions of interest to wealthier individuals than to questions of interest to poor individuals. We believe this reflects the fact that mayors themselves tend to come from wealthier backgrounds, allowing them to have firsthand experience with, say, a high school's advanced placement program

but not with the school's free lunch program. Consistent with this explanation, we find that a mayor's likelihood of responding to our questions was
moderated by the wealth of the city. The wealthier the city, the more likely
the mayor was to answer a question about advanced placement courses and
the less likely the mayor was to answer a question about free lunch programs.
Taken together, the evidence shows that descriptive representation can matter
because of the knowledge that representatives bring to office. One reason that
underrepresented groups are disadvantaged is that fewer public officials have
personal experience with, and thus information about, the issues important to
them.

Chapter 6
In Chapter 6, two large-scale constituency service field experiments show that
legislators exhibit bias against racial minorities when deciding which constituents to help. Further, the experiments show that descriptive representation helps mitigate this bias because state legislators are more responsive to
constituents from their own racial or ethnic groups. This result holds across
parties. There is also evidence that legislators use the additional information
about the senders' likely partisanship and their likelihood of turning out to
vote. However, the preference that legislators show for constituents from their
own racial or ethnic groups cannot be explained by legislators using race or
ethnicity to infer constituents' partisan preferences, likelihood of turning out,
or SES. Instead, the increased responsiveness seems to be driven by legislators'
preferences.

   I conduct a similar experiment to test for gender bias in legislators' output
and do not find any. Further, there is no evidence that descriptive representation matters by gender; male and female legislators treat male and female
constituents similarly. There is evidence that an in-group preference by race
and ethnicity directly affects politicians' outputs, but there is no comparable
bias related to gender or SES (shown in Chapter 5).

Chapter 7
My experiments confirm that at least part of the bias in representation is
explained by the fact that politicians come to office with information, attitudes,
and preferences that drive their behavior. Further, politicians' backgrounds
lead to bias both because of the personal biases that elected officials bring
to office and because they are strategic actors seeking to be reelected. The
information that legislators bring to office incentivizes them to focus more
than they otherwise would on the issues of interest to voters like them.

   Significantly, the direct bias that legislators bring to office affects different
groups in different ways. Officials are more likely to discount the intensity and
thoughtfulness of low-income constituents' opinions, but they do not exhibit a
direct personal bias against them when creating policy outcomes. The reverse
is true for racial and ethnic minorities. Officials do not discount the opinions

of racial minorities, but the non-Latino white legislators, who represent the majority of legislators in the United States, do exhibit a personal bias in favor of white constituents. There is no gender bias at either of these stages of the process. The difference in bias across groups has implications for understanding which institutions can be used to mitigate bias against disadvantaged groups. In the conclusion I discuss these institutions and the implications of the results for political science.

When Can Representation Break Down?

Politicians are not completely adaptable actors who come to office as blank slates (Burden 2007 and the review therein). Instead, politicians' backgrounds influence their behavior in office, which, in turn, leads to bias in at least two ways.

First, elected officials who want to maximize their chances of winning should focus on the issues that they are most informed about. They should work on these issues because it is less costly to do so and therefore a more efficient way to achieve their reelection goals. Because politicians' own backgrounds are an important determinant of the knowledge and experience that politicians have, voters who are numerically underrepresented in office are disadvantaged because the issues they care about receive less attention.

Second, bias can arise because legislators come to office with personal biases. These biases can affect the representation process both at the input stage of the policy-making process, when politicians consider constituents' opinions, and directly at the output stage of the process. Some groups may be under-represented because public officials are simply biased against them when they create policy and other outputs. Studying the inequality of representation at these parts of the process allows me to see where political inequality arises for various groups.

Other Parts of the Representation Process

These aspects of the representation process do not constitute an exhaustive description of that process. Most prominently, prior research has focused on the differences in groups' rates of political participation (e.g., Verba and Nie 1972; Piven and Cloward 1988; Rosenstone and Hansen 1993; Verba, Schlozman, and Brady 1995; Lijphart 1997).

I focus on these aspects of the process, however, because they provide the best opportunity to test the claim that politicians' backgrounds lead to inequality in representation. These are the points in the process where politicians take direct action. By studying politicians' direct actions we can see whether they act evenhandedly with different constituents. Despite the importance of directly studying politicians' behavior, scholars have given much less attention to how politicians respond to the inputs or messages they receive from constituents. As Sidney Verba puts it, "The literature on the receipt of messages and the response to them is not as well developed as that on the messages sent" (2003, 666).

One of the contributions of this book is that I study what happens after constituents share their inputs or messages with politicians. This allows me to study how politicians' backgrounds lead to breakdowns in representation for different groups of voters.

Bias in Information: The Effect of Legislators' Background on Their Proactive Behavior

Because politicians' time is scarce, the cost of becoming informed shapes their behavior, especially with regard to items requiring proactive effort. Kingdon (1981) highlighted the importance of information costs in shaping legislators' behavior. Drawing on earlier work by Cyert and March (1963), Kingdon argued that legislators "dramatically reduce the necessity to search out and examine information by limiting their searches only to those decisions which they have some kind of problem or difficulty in making. For the rest of their decisions, their search for information is rudimentary at best, and perhaps altogether absent" (228). Because becoming informed takes time and resources, legislators necessarily have to limit the effort they make to invest in becoming informed. For roll call votes, the rank-and-file legislators have no control over the agenda and so must decide on issues that lie outside their expertise. However, legislators choose the issue areas they will pursue proactively, and the argument behind the lower informational cost mechanism is simply that legislators will be more active on issues where it is less costly for them to work.

The personal experiences that politicians bring to office are a source of bias because they lead politicians to put more effort into issues that people like them know the most about. The rationale is simple: politicians have limited time to spend in serving their constituents' interests while pursuing their own reelection goals. As Hall and Deardoff (2006) put it, politicians "have limited capacity – in time, information, labor, and hence agenda space – to address the numerous issues on which the legislator wants to be involved" (72). Given such limitations, legislators strategically concentrate their efforts in areas yielding the greatest electoral return while expending the least amount of effort. If politicians have information and experiences that make it less costly to work on a given issue, they will, ceteris paribus, work on that issue more. As a result of this dynamic, politicians should naturally engage more proactively with issues that constituents who are like them care about, in drafting legislation, giving speeches, investigating issues, and dealing with constituents.

A simple decision-theoretic model formalizes this point. Assume that politicians have to choose how much effort they will put into two different issues, A and B. Voters reward them for their efforts on these issues, which we can generically represent with the following utility function for the politician:

$$U = F(w_A, w_B) \tag{1}$$

My argument is that the amount of work one does on an issue (i.e., w_i) is a function of the time a politician puts into the issue and the level of information the politician has on the issue. To see this, let e_i indicate the experience and skill that a politician has with issue i (and thus, his or her level of information about the issue). When legislators have more information about an issue, they can be more efficient when working on that issue and get more done in less time (Hall and Deardoff 2006). I indicate the politician's skill on an issue A *relative* to issue B as $x = \frac{e_A}{e_A+e_B}$. Further, define t as the percentage of their available time that they choose to work on issue A, and $1-t$ as the percentage of available time they will work on issue B. Given the utility function in Equation 1, politicians should use all the time they have available to achieve their reelection goal and should not waste any time. Hence, time is a crucial constraint and is also the factor that politicians control. Finally, I express the outcomes w_A and w_B as production functions that yield the following outcomes:

$$w_A = (t)^x; \quad w_B = (1-t)^{1-x} \tag{2}$$

Thus the payoff for time spent working on an issue depends on the relative weight that voters put on that issue and legislators' information about that issue (which measures how efficient they are). Expressing the production functions in these terms allows us to get Equation 3, which is just a variant of the Cobb-Douglas[1]:

$$U = F(w_A, w_B) = t^x(1-t)^{(1-x)} \tag{3}$$

Taking the derivative of politician's utility function (i.e., Equation 3) with respect to t shows that the optimal amount time spent on issue A, t^*, for the politician is (the calculation for this result is provided in the Chapter Appendix):

$$t^* = x \tag{4}$$

Equation 4 shows that the optimal amount of time to put into an issue increases with one's relative knowledge (or skill) related to that issue (i.e., t increases with x). Politicians will put more effort into issue area A when

---

[1] This formulation reflects a situation where voters value having some effort put into a combination of the two issues over a situation where only one issue receives all of the attention.

they have more knowledge about that issue, and more effort into issue area B when they have more knowledge in that area. Legislators' personal experiences incentivize them to play to their comparative advantage and deal with those issues they know best as it represents the most efficient way to secure votes for a given level of effort.[2]

This argument should not be caricatured. It does not mean they will work on an issue if relatively few of their constituents care about that issue. If there is no political return for working on issue B, then politicians will not work on that issue no matter how efficiently they can do so. However, when deciding how to allocate time across different issues that voters care about – politicians will, all else equal, play to their strengths and focus on issues where they have greater levels of prior knowledge.

Legislators' Background as a Key Source of Information

A key argument of this book is that the legislators' own backgrounds are an important source for the information that determines their ability to work on different issues. In his own interview work, Burden (2007) found that several former legislators expressed these sentiments. Two former educators, for example, suggested that their prior background prepared them to work actively on education issues. Phil Sharp, a former college professor, said, "[T]hose things in my background always came into play in my ability to talk about things . . . so it's not like they were dead. Like with education, I was able to talk about things." Connie Morrella, who had also been a teacher, cited her ability to "call on [her] experiences as an educator" when considering education issues. Both felt that they could use the information they gained from their own backgrounds to be proactively involved in issues involving education even without being involved with the education committee.

Because information is also gleaned as part of our life experiences, politicians will put more effort into working on issues related to their demographic characteristics (Bratton and Haynie 1999; Swers 2002). Legislators have more knowledge about these issues, and so they can work on them more efficiently. In the aggregate, this will create a dynamic in which the issues that are important to numerically underrepresented groups will simply receive less attention from politicians.

Complementary Forms of Information-Induced Bias in Representation

It is worth noting that there are other ways in which information can affect and bias representation. The most prominent argument about information is that

---

[2] While the exact dynamics will depend on how the model is formalized, simple extensions suggest that information will lead to a greater amount of bias when there are relatively large numbers of voters who care about the issue. Thus it is constituents in the numerical minority who will particularly suffer if elected politicians do not have information about their issue.

it affects the quality of deliberation. Jane Mansbridge (1999; see also Hoffman and Maier 1961; van Knippenberg, De Dreu, and Homan 2004), for example, argues that descriptive representation is particularly beneficial when legislative bodies deliberate on new issues for which constituents do not have definitely formed opinions.

When this is the case, individuals for whom these relatively uncrystallized interests are extremely important may get their best substantive representation from a descriptive representative. Here, the important communication is not vertical, between the representation and constituent, but horizontal, among deliberating legislators. In this horizontal communication, a descriptive representative can draw on elements of experiences shared with constituents to explore the uncharted ramifications of newly presented issues and also to speak on those issues with a voice carrying the authority of experience. (644)

Justice Stevens, in his dissenting opinion on *Miller v. Johnson* (1995), makes a similar argument for the benefits of electing a diverse set of representatives. At issue in *Miller* was whether Georgia's newly created Eleventh District was constitutional. It was an unusually shaped district, stretching over six thousand miles. The *Almanac of American Politics* described the geography of the Eleventh District as "a monstrosity" (Barone and Ujifusa 1995: 356). The state legislature drew this district to create three majority-black districts and receive preclearance from the Department of Justice, which had rejected two earlier plans that only included two majority-black districts. While the court ruled against the district, Justice Stevens defended the plan with three majority-black districts: "The districting plan here," he opined, "serves the interest in diversity and tolerance by increasing the likelihood that a meaningful number of black representatives will add their voices to legislative debates."

And in summing up the literature on this topic, Swers and Rouse (2011) wrote:

Within the legislature, political theorists assert that the election of descriptive representatives will have important effects on the nature and quality of deliberation among legislators and the substantive representation of group interests in the content of policy outputs. On the basis of shared experiences, descriptive representatives will bring new issues to the congressional agenda and will provide a different perspective on more established debates by delineating how those issues will differentially impact members of the underrepresented group. (244)

This insight-based argument complements the efficiency-driven argument I am making. The insight-based argument suggests that bias arises because the legislature as a whole will have less expertise to draw on when making decisions for numerically underrepresented groups. The efficiency-driven argument reaches the same conclusion but for a different, though complementary, reason. I argue that information leads to bias because it incentivizes politicians to focus on issues they know the most about. If we miss this dynamic and only focus on the bias related to the quality of deliberation, we will underestimate the bias that numerically underrepresented groups face.

Bias in Processing Constituents' Opinions

I also test how politicians' personal biases affect both the input and output stages of the representation process. I study bias at the input stage by testing whether elected officials discount some constituents' opinions more than others. In extensive interviews with members of Congress (MCs), Kingdon (1981) suggested two different ways in which politicians might rationalize giving less weight to some constituents' opinions.

First, politicians might rationalize that some constituents care less about the issue. Constituents' level of interest in an issue is important because politicians have incentives to be more responsive to voters who care deeply about issues. Research on issue publics suggests that voters who care more about an issue are more likely to know what actions legislators take on the issue and hold them accountable for those actions (Converse 1964; Krosnick 1990; Iyengar et al. 2008). For some voters who care deeply about an issue, no other issues matter. One of the legislators that Fenno interviewed stated, "There isn't one voter in 20,000 who knows my voting record, except on that one thing that affects him" (1978: 142).

Some views of representation suggest that politicians should in fact be more responsive to individuals who feel strongly about an issue. Theorists arguing for pluralism, for example, suggest that there are multiple centers of political power, with different groups of voters influencing policies in the areas about which they care more deeply than other voters do (Dahl 1967).

Regardless of one's position on pluralism, there is evidence that legislators are in fact more responsive to people who feel strongly about an issue (e.g., Wlezien 2004). Kingdon (1981), in his study of what influences MCs' votes, highlights constituents' intensity as a major factor determining politicians' responsiveness to public opinion.

When the congressman feels strongly [about an issue] and his constituents do not, he will prefer his own feeling, since his constituents, while having an opinion contrary to his, do not feel particularly strongly about the matter. When the congressman does not feel very strongly about the matter but his constituents do, he is likely to go along with them. (38)

Because legislators are more responsive to constituents with intense preferences, politicians will be less responsive to constituents who (they think) do not care much about the issue.

I also test for a second type of rationalization – that public officials assume that some constituents understand less about the issue. Gerber, Huber, Doherty, and Dowling (2011) present a decision-theoretic model of voters' utility in which the impact of a candidate's policy position on voters' utility depends on how confident they are that their own position represents the correct position. The authors then show that voters recognize that "their expertise varies across policy domains when deciding whether to act on those opinions to evaluate elected officials" (1221). Their experimental tests show that voters are in fact more willing to punish a legislator for his or her position when they are more confident about their own ability to evaluate the policy proposal. Consequently, politicians should expect less retribution from voters when they deviate from voters' preferred policies if they think the voters are less confident about their own positions on the issue.

It may also be that legislators believe they can change their constituents' positions. Explaining their votes to constituents is an important part of what legislators do. As Fenno writes, legislators "cast a certain vote only when they are convinced that they have a satisfactory explanation in hand" (1978, 141).

Some believe that politicians use these explanations for their own cynical purposes. Jacobs and Shapiro (2000; see also Jacobs et al. 1998), for example, argue that politicians develop these explanations by following poll results "in order to identify the words, arguments, and symbols that are most likely to be effective in attracting favorable press coverage and ultimately 'winning' public support for their desired policies" (Jacobs and Shapiro 2000, 7). The authors argue that politicians are extremely effective in using these strategies and that this leads them to pursue their own policy agendas: "Politicians' attempts to change public sentiment toward their favored position convinces them that they can pursue their policy objectives while minimizing the risks of electoral punishment" (7).

On the other hand, some argue that politicians use these explanations to try to educate the public. In his own work, Fenno met a member who argued that he had "the best platform from which to educate of anyone in the country. To me, there's no difference between leadership and education. You know what the Latin mean of education is – 'to lead out.' What is politics if not teaching?" (1978, 162).

Whether their motives are nefarious or not, politicians are in a position to explain their positions to constituents. This ability to provide an explanation is also the ability to lead opinion on the issue (Gabel and Scheve 2007). Thus, if elected officials think that constituents are misinformed, they may believe that constituents are likely to come around to their way of thinking when they learn more about the issue.

In sum, groups may be underrepresented if elected officials discount their opinions by rationalizing that individuals belonging to that group may not be as well informed or feel as intensely about the issue as other individuals do.

Why Focus on These Two Rationalizations?

I focus on the role of issue salience and issue information because the literature on representation suggests that these are the important considerations that politicians take into account when reaching decisions (see the earlier discussion). There are other ways, of course, public officials might rationalize ignoring constituents' opinions. Motivated reasoning, for example, has played an important role in understanding bias in voter decision making (Lodge and

Taber 2000; Redlawsk 2002). Future work could also study whether other cognitive biases, such as motivated reasoning, are at play. Such biases, if they are operative, should reinforce the biases uncovered here.

Direct Group Bias in Outputs

Elected officials may also engage in bias against a given group (and/or exhibit favoritism toward another group) when creating outputs for strategic reasons or because of their personal biases. For example, Republicans may be less responsive to racial minorities because racial minorities are more likely to vote Democratic, and therefore they may believe that their efforts to help minorities are less likely to yield electoral returns. Alternatively, they may be less responsive to racial minorities simply because they do not want to help them. Because the range of policy solutions available to mitigate bias depends on the underlying motivation, I design experiments to separate biases driven by politicians' personal preferences and those driven by their strategic considerations.

In Chapter 6, I focus on identifying politicians' nonstrategic bias without further delineating the motive. Researchers have in fact identified various motives for such bias, including out-group prejudice, in-group favoritism, and linked fate. These motives are very different, but the consequence is the same: one's in-group receives better treatment. I simply use the term *personal preference* to indicate a nonstrategic motive.

The term *personal preference* has the advantage of being flexible enough to travel across different contexts. One of the advantages of this research program is that I test for bias that different groups might face. While it is possible that both women and racial minorities face bias because of elected officials' personal preferences, there are reasons to expect that this bias might be driven by different motives. The term *personal preference* is flexible enough to apply to the various underlying motives that might be at play while still emphasizing that this bias is not driven by strategic considerations.

Strategic considerations can drive output-stage bias because politicians try to use information to selectively target constituents. Fenno observed that "every member has some idea of the people most likely to join his reelection constituency. . . . During a campaign these people will often be 'targeted' and subjected to special recruiting or activating efforts" (1978, 9). Similarly, Bartels writes that "rational candidates are impelled by the goal of vote maximization to discriminate among prospective voters, appealing primarily to those who either are likely to vote and susceptible to partisan conversion or reliable supporters susceptible to mobilization (or likely opponents susceptible to demobilization)" (1998, 68; see also Hamburger and Wallsten 2005; Jacobs and Shapiro 2005; Hillygus and Shields 2008).

Strategic targeting could lead to bias against a group if constituents' demographic characteristics are correlated with politically relevant information such as a constituent's partisanship or likelihood of voting. Imagine, for example, that individuals' SES is observed but their propensity to turn out to vote is not. If some constituents are less likely to vote, legislators might strategically put less effort into helping them because their preferences are less likely to affect the election. If representatives believe that low-income individuals are less likely to vote, they might engage in strategic discrimination and be less helpful to the poor because they are focusing on voters who are more likely to vote.

Legislators' Strategic Considerations in the Constituency Service Field Experiments

The constituency field experiments that I present highlight why it is important to try to control for these strategic factors. In the 2010 race experiment I conducted (see Chapter 6), a third of the legislators in the study received e-mails from people stating that they were members of the legislator's party but typically did not vote. Legislators noticed this information, and some made overt appeals to the correspondent to vote as part of their response. For example:

I am saddened to hear that you don't usually vote. I hope that I can encourage you to do so in the future. I must confess that I was not always as diligent as I am now about exercising my voting privileges. Since joining the legislature six years ago and acquiring a fuller picture of the legislation that is introduced each year as well as how that legislation affects my entire extended family as well as all of our citizens, I am much more committed to doing so. If you need any assistance in registering to vote we would be happy to provide information that may be of help to you.

PLEASE VOTE this year – this is the most important election in a long time and we need to AT LEAST have a republican Governor.

I would be honored to have your Vote!

I hope that you will register to vote and will support keeping the Democratic majority in the state. We need to continue with the progress that we have made in the last several years.

Legislators care about voters' partisan loyalties and their propensity to turn out to vote.

Differentiating between Personal Preferences and Strategic Discrimination

Differentiating between personal preferences and strategic discrimination can be difficult, as both models predict that legislators will pay more attention to some constituents than others. In many ways identifying a particular form of strategic discrimination is easier. In my experiments I randomize two dimensions of the e-mails that were sent to legislators (Chapter 6 provides the text of the e-mails): the group the message is sent from, in this case the race or ethnicity of the letter writer; and whether the message contains the information the legislator might be inferring from the writer's group membership. When the information is not provided to the public official, the difference between the two groups includes both the strategic discrimination based on the information that is being experimentally manipulated and any residual discrimination. When the information is provided, only residual discrimination should drive any observed differential treatment. Thus, the difference-in-differences isolates the strategic discrimination due to the public official using the letter writer's race, gender, or income to make inferences about the letter writer.

Convincingly identifying bias driven by personal preferences is more difficult. Recent field experiments measuring labor market discrimination have focused on randomizing names on the resumes of various job applicants (e.g., Bertrand and Mullainathan 2004; Adida, Laitin, and Valfort 2010). This approach holds constant relevant facts about the applicants' skills and qualifications, such as their levels of education and experience. Using this approach, Bertrand and Mullainathan (2004) find that job applicants with black-sounding names are less likely to get offers for job interviews even when the resumes indicate that the candidates are of equal quality. The authors conclude that this is evidence of racial discrimination in the labor market. However, Fryer and Levitt (2004) have criticized their findings, arguing that the artifacts of social class implied by the distinctively racial names used in these studies may have driven the results. In relation to the investigation here, Fryer and Levitt's more general point is that the bias attributed to personal preferences may in fact be another form of strategic discrimination. This is a general empirical hurdle faced by studies of discrimination.

We can still learn about discrimination, however, by testing for evidence of the types of strategic discrimination described earlier. Further, we can include the relevant information that we think legislators might be inferring from an individual's group identity directly in the message. If we include the relevant information, the residual differential treatment can be attributed to the official's personal biases. I test whether there is evidence of discrimination after controlling for the potentially important sources of strategic discrimination, specifically designing my constituency service field experiments to rule out the possibility that legislators are simply using demographic characteristics to make inferences about a constituent's partisanship or likelihood of voting.

Testing for In-Group Bias

In many of the experiments, I test whether legislators exhibit a personal preference for helping people like themselves. When I investigate whether public officials favor people like themselves due to their personal biases, I use the phrase *in-group, personal preference*. That said, nothing precludes the possibility that politicians will favor people outside their own demographic groups. I focus on in-group bias because it may explain why numerically underrepresented groups are disadvantaged. It also has implications for whether or not increasing descriptive representation can mitigate some of the bias faced by disadvantaged groups. In the next chapter I turn to explaining some of the experiments used to test for this bias.

Chapter 2 Appendix

Solving for the Optimal Allocation of Time across Issues

Equation 3 gave the politician's utility function as follows:

$$U = t^x(1 - t)^{(1-x)} \tag{5}$$

Taking the derivative of Equation 5 with respect to t and applying the product rule gives the following result:

$$\frac{\partial}{\partial t}U = t^x \left(\frac{\partial}{\partial t}(1 - t)^{(1-x)}\right) + xt^{x-1}(1 - t)^{(1-x)} \tag{6}$$

Applying the chain rule to the first element of Equation 6 yields Equation 7:

$$\frac{\partial}{\partial t}U = -t^x(1 - x)(1 - t)^{-x} + xt^{x-1}(1 - t)^{(1-x)} \tag{7}$$

Setting Equation 7 equal to zero, we can solve the optimal level of t (given as t^*):

$$t^{*x}(1 - x)(1 - t^*)^{-x} = xt^{*x-1}(1 - t^*)^{(1-x)} \tag{8}$$

$$(1 - x)t^* = x(1 - t^*) \tag{9}$$

$$t^* - xt^* = x - xt^* \tag{10}$$

$$t^* = x \tag{11}$$

Equation 11 is the optimal solution presented in Equation 4.

3

Details of the Constituency Service Field Experiments

In this chapter I discuss some of the common features of the constituency service field experiments that I present in Chapters 5 and 6. In my experiments I measure how public officials respond to short, simple constituency service requests that are sent via e-mail (e.g., requests for information about schools). I then measure various dimensions of the quality of the response. These experiments are of a type often referred to as an audit study. I discuss the general considerations for these audit studies because, despite their power, they are not widely used in political science. Specific details of each experiment are given in the chapter where it is used.

Experimenting on Whom?

One key feature of my experiments is that I study elites to increase the external validity of the results. The utility of experimentation depends on both its internal validity (the degree to which the experiment can identify the cause-effect relationship under investigation) and its external validity (the degree to which the findings are informative about contexts outside the experiment). The ability to randomly assign participants to treatment and control conditions helps ensure that the studies are internally valid, but it does not guarantee that the experiments are externally valid. Most experiments in political science are conducted in lab settings using paid participants, typically undergraduate students. Researchers expose these students to stimuli to try to learn how individuals outside the lab would react to similar stimuli. In most cases, lab participants likely provide a good view of how well-informed voters act in the real world. But it is less likely that such experiments can provide information about how public officials are likely to behave (Sears 1986; McDermott 2002, 2013; Butler and Kousser 2013). For my studies, I directly experiment on the offices of public officials in the conduct of their regular duties, strengthening the external validity of the results.

I study politicians' offices because this is the level at which many of the decisions that affect representation are made. In practice, the response to communications with the offices may have come from staff members and not necessarily the elected officials; not surprisingly, whether or not the response seems to have been written by a staff member depends on how professionalized the office is (Squire 1992, 2007).[1] For state legislators in more professionalized states, such as California and New York, a staff member clearly deals with communications. However, legislators from less professionalized states and most mayors I study appear to write the responses themselves. This is especially true for communications sent to state legislators when the legislature is out of session.

However, even when staff members write the responses, the experiments are informative about how public officials represent their constituents. Because I use the representatives' official e-mail addresses, responses to the communications are made on behalf of the public officials. Further, elected officials rely on staff to help in all aspects of their work. Salisbury and Shepsle (1981a,b) argue that the legislator's enterprise, which includes staff members serving as agents with the legislator as principal, is the relevant unit for legislative decision making. Thus learning about responsiveness, regardless of who writes the response, is informative of the elected official's enterprise. The offices where staff members are more likely to respond to constituent communication are also the offices where staff members are more likely to participate in other aspects of official duties, such as research on legislation or speech writing. Thus the determinants of responsiveness tell us about the way the elected official's office prioritizes other aspects of its work.

Experiments as a Measurement Tool

I conduct these audit studies on elected officials' enterprises in order *to measure their behavior, not change their behavior*. The most prominent audit study in political science comes from Robert Putnam's seminal book *Making Democracy Work* (1993, 73). Putnam and his collaborators measured bureaucratic efficiency across the Italian regions by sending several requests to bureaucrats in each region and measuring their responsiveness. These researchers were trying to measure bureaucrats' behavior, not change it. I do the same.

Some Ethical Considerations in Experimenting on Public Officials

Field experiments are becoming increasingly common in political science, but field experiments on public officials by academics are relatively rare (exceptions

---

[1] While professionalism affects who responds, it does not affect the overall results. David Broockman and I (2011) found no evidence for a heterogeneous treatment effect in more highly professionalized legislatures. Thus the behavior among state legislators that I uncover in this book should apply to state legislators from all states.

include Putnam 1993; Bergan 2009; Butler and Nickerson 2011; Butler, Karpowitz, and Pope 2012).[2] Because of the rarity of such experiments, I discuss here some of the major ethical considerations that went into the experimental design and explain how those considerations shaped the experiments. My hope is that researchers will engage in such introspection before experimenting on public officials – and that researchers using more traditional observational, survey, and interview methods will include similar considerations in their work because these issues are not unique to experiments (Dexter 1964).

First, the use of deception should be minimized as much as possible. I used fictitious aliases when contacting legislators and experimentally manipulated the information conveyed. It is possible to get actual individuals to contact public officials and express their own opinions (see Butler, Karpowitz, and Pope 2012), but this approach limits the questions that can be asked. The experiments that try to differentiate between strategic and nonstrategic motivations for bias are typically only feasible with fictitious individuals, where information such as partisanship can be randomly assigned (see, e.g., Chapter 6). This is why fictitious names and resumes are used in similar studies of labor market discrimination (e.g., Adida, Laitin, and Valfort 2010). Similarly, the studies comparing the behavior of mayors (see Chapter 5) were only feasible on a large scale using aliases. Some deception was thus necessary for this particular experiment. While researchers should be able to use deception, they should minimize its use when possible (McDermott 2013).

Second, I tried to minimize any harm that might come from the experiments. I took steps to maintain the anonymity of officials' responses to ensure that the experiments were not used to tarnish reputations. This differs from the approaches of some partisan activists and journalists, who use deception to gain access to public officials. When a liberal blogger records a call between himself, posing as an important Republican donor, and Wisconsin's republican governor (Marley, Glauber, and Schultze 2011) or a conservative activist videotapes sting operations between his confederates and representatives from the Association of Community Organizations for Reform Now (ACORN) and National Public Radio (Rainey 2011), the individuals behind those operations are trying to highlight the behavior of particular individuals. In contrast, I am trying to learn about systematic differences among elected officials as a whole.

It also would be misleading, from a scientific perspective, to report the behavior of a specific legislator. Because we do not observe all potential outcomes – the response to a request from members of all racial, ethnic, or gender groups – for any given legislator, we do not know how he or she would have responded to other treatments. We can only make average comparisons across groups of legislators.

---

[2] Indeed, most of the field experiments on public officials have been funded and conducted by federal agencies to audit whether government programs discriminate on the basis of race (Fix and Turner 1998; see especially Chapter 6).

Finally, I considered how to minimize the burden placed on legislators' time. In doing so I tried to meet Putnam's standard when he described his own experiment as "slightly deceptive, but innocuous and highly informative" (1993, 73). Some burden was necessary because, as Hall (1996) suggests, seeing how legislators choose to expend time and effort is the best way to learn about their priorities. That said, I tried to choose requests that would be fairly easy to respond to so I would not prevent legislators from working for their constituents.[3]

Keeping the text of the e-mails simple and generic also highlights how stark the existing political inequality is. The minimal nature of the e-mails means that we can attribute the results of the audit studies to the feature of the e-mail we are changing (usually the characteristic of who sent the e-mail). This type of control is one of the advantages of the experimental design. In practice, janitors and lawyers might use different language when they write, but in the experiment the e-mails from these two groups are the same. Thus we know that it is the profession of the writer, and not the content, that is driving any differences in how public officials respond.

Why State and Local Officials?

In designing the experiments I draw on the strengths of studying both Congress and state and local officials. One advantage to studying Congress is that the political science literature on representation and Congress is more developed. I draw on this literature heavily as I design and analyze the experiments. However, two downsides to studying Congress are, first, there are fewer MCs and, second, we have less access to them. The advantage of studying state and local officials is that there are many more politicians to study and we have access to these officials.

The studies in Chapter 6, for example, highlight the advantage of including a large number of politicians at the state and local level. In that chapter I examine whether legislators are more responsive to constituents from their own racial or ethnic group. Studying this question at the federal level would effectively limit the question to the behavior of white legislators. (As of writing, there are only forty-three black legislators and twenty-four Latino legislators in the U.S. Congress.) With sample sizes that small we cannot confidently test whether minority legislators in Congress show a preference for members of their own

---

[3] Based on the responses received, I believe that the studies succeeded. In the 2008 race study (see Chapter 6), the median reply of the replies that we received (nearly half of the legislative offices did not reply) was 291 characters long. Assuming an average word length of 5 characters plus a space after each word, the median message was only 49 words long, roughly the length of the remainder of this paragraph. I believe that these experiments caused no significant harm either to the state legislators who were our subjects or to constituents who were seeking their help at the time.

groups. Among state legislators, however, there are about six hundred black legislators and over one hundred Latino legislators, allowing me to study the way both white and minority legislators represent their constituents. There are similar advantages to studying gender and descriptive representation at the state level.

The experiments in Chapter 4 show the advantage that comes with having greater access to state legislators. Researchers do not have the access necessary to get enough MCs to participate in the type of survey experiments presented in that chapter. However because we have greater access to state legislators and local officials, I am able to use the survey experiments in Chapter 4 to test whether elected officials discount the opinions of different groups.

There are, of course, important differences between Congress and state and local officials that should attenuate the degree to which the bias we uncover here should also apply to the behavior of MCs. One reason why MCs might exhibit less bias in their communications with constituents is that they face more scrutiny by the media. Members of Congress also have a larger number of constituents and more resources than state and local officials do. In practice they can use these resources to organize their offices as bureaucratic machines: a letter comes in, a letter goes out, with the routine nature of the office process overriding potential differences across letters. In other words, congressional offices should be less likely to differentiate among the communications they receive.

Chris Karpowitz, Jeremy Pope, and I (Butler, Karpowitz, and Pope 2012) ran a constituency field experiment in 2008 that confirms that MCs are less likely than state legislators to differentiate among the communications they receive. We recruited over two hundred participants to write letters to their representatives in Congress and their state legislatures. Participants wrote two sets of letters. One set asked for a simple constituency service request, and one set asked the legislator about his or her policy position on an issue. We then randomized which type of letter was sent to each of the roughly one thousand legislators in the sample. Because we sent the same types of letters to both MCs and members of the state legislature, we can compare their relative levels of responsiveness.

Both federal and state legislators were more responsive to service requests than policy requests, but the difference was especially pronounced among state legislators. State legislators were approximately thirty-two percentage points less responsive to policy letters; they responded to 51 percent of the service requests and 19 percent of the policy requests. Members of Congress however, were only fourteen percentage points less responsive to policy letters; they responded to 52 percent of the service letters and 38 percent of the policy letters. The difference in differences between state and federal legislators is statistically significant. If we used the behavior of MCs to infer how state legislators behaved, we would underestimate the degree to which state legislators differentiated between the letters they received.

The results from that same study also support the claim that we can learn about MCs by studying the behavior of local officials. The MCs and state legislators exhibited bias in the same direction (only the magnitude of the measured bias was different).

One reason that we can learn about MCs from the behavior of state legislators is that state governments are patterned after the federal government. As a result, state legislatures share many of their most important institutional design features with Congress, including separation of powers, regular elections, and bicameralism.

Further, the majority of MCs served in their respective state legislatures before going to Congress. Fully 46 percent of U.S. senators and 50 percent of U.S. House members had previously served as state legislators (National Conference of State Legislatures 2013). Service in the state legislature is a training ground for congressional service. Studying the behavior of state legislators provides insights into the behavior of MCs early in their careers.

That is not to say that we should abandon the study of either group. We need to study both. In fact when there are relevant differences between federal and state legislators or legislative institutions, it is inappropriate to use state legislators to test theories that have been developed with respect to Congress. However, for many questions, there are great advantages to using state legislators to study theoretical questions that have been developed to explain congressional behavior and outcomes (Butler and Powell 2014).

Even if the results I show can only be applied to state and local officials, they provide an important contribution because these officials play a substantial role in determining the tax and spending policies that significantly affect constituents (Tax Policy Center 2013). State and local governments are responsible for a large proportion of public expenditures, hire the majority of government employees, and deal with the issues that citizens care most about (Trounstine 2009; Arnold and Carnes 2012).

Why Use E-mail?

Using e-mail in the experiments provides greater external validity because e-mail communication is the most common way that citizens contact their elected officials. In their survey of citizens, the Congressional Management Foundation (Goldschmidt and Ochreiter 2008) found that 32 percent of the people who contacted an MC used e-mail. Another 7 percent used the webform on the member's website. By comparison, 24 percent of the respondents called the legislator's office and 18 percent sent a letter by postal mail.

Measuring Legislative Responsiveness

In addition to measuring whether an official responded, I measured aspects of the quality of the response because not all responses were equally helpful. In some cases the responses were even abrasive. One legislator in the 2008 race study (see Chapter 6) wrote the following to a putative black constituent seeking to learn about the registration process.

Mr. Jackson:

You may register legally at your county clerk's office in the county of your residence. Or, if you wish to be registered at some residence for which you are not legally qualified, wish to register after the deadline, or become a voter in any other unlawful way, you can contact Mr. Obama's group, ACORN, and they will register you regardless of your qualifications.

Cordially,
[redacted]

This e-mail was a dramatic exception to the genuinely cordial tone of most responses. Still, not all the legislators provided useful information. In response to an e-mail asking for information about laws regulating breast-feeding at work, one legislator responded with a two-word message: "Try Google."

Of course even short e-mails can be informative. One public official who was asked about laws regarding smoking in public areas responded with a three-word message that was short and straight to the point: "Don't do it."

Still, it is clear that not all officials put the same amount of effort into responding to the e-mails. The following four responses illustrate the range of effort that different officials went to in order to help the constituents.

I don't have any information on this program. Sorry I cant help.

I don't know the answers to either of your questions. Call the DMV regarding the second question and call the Governor's Office regarding your first question.

Thank you for your email. I appreciate that you have take the time to write.

I am forwarding your email to [a member of the state Department of Education] and will ask her to provide you with assistance per your request.

I also found this site [redacted]. It contains some information regarding school comparisons that may be helpful.

If you have any questions, please give me a call at [redacted] or email.
Sincerely,
[redacted]

Thank you for your e-mail. I just spoke with the Secretary of State's office and was informed that . . . [here the legislator gave a paragraph on steps that had to be taken].

Although none of the legislators knew the response to the question he or she was asked when the e-mail was first received, some made an effort to become informed.

In addition to looking at whether the elected official responded, I include two measures for the quality of the response, producing three outcomes for the constituency service field experiments presented throughout the book. *Responded* measures whether the official provided any type of personal response to the e-mail (this does not include automatically generated responses or newsletters). *Timely response* measures whether the official's personal response arrived within two weeks of the date when the original e-mail was sent; those who took longer than two weeks to respond and those who did not respond at all are coded the same way. *Answered question* measures whether the official's response answered the question that was asked; those who did not respond at all and those who responded but did not answer the question are coded the same way.

I use the last two outcomes to indicate the quality of the response. They are coded so that those who provide a low-quality response, in terms of the dimension measured, are grouped together with those who do not respond at all. I make this comparison rather than comparing the quality of responses across treatments among those who respond because self-selection potentially biases any measures that only uses the sample of those who respond (see the discussions in McConnell, Stuart, and Devaney 2008; Angrist and Pischke 2009, 94–110). Finally, because all the hypotheses I test predict that effects should go in a specific direction, I use one-tailed tests for all the analyses.

Why Not Use Roll Call Votes to Study This Question?

There are several advantages to studying constituency communication instead of roll call votes. First, roll call votes can be problematic because groups do not necessarily have monolithic preferences and there are often complex policy interests in play and confounding variables present (see the discussion in Griffin and Newman 2007). These factors make it difficult to determine whether representatives are acting in a group's interest. In contrast, it is easy to measure whether representatives are acting in the interest of someone contacting them with a question. Surveys show that over 90 percent of citizens, even those who are just contacting their public officials in order to register their opinions, desire a response (Goldschmidt and Ochreiter 2008). Because the e-mails in my experiments specifically ask for help, the interests of persons contacting a public official are clear and straightforward: they want a response.

Second, response rates can be compared explicitly across groups to see whether representatives treat them differently. Many researchers study how well a given group is represented but fail to gauge the relative level of representation. For instance, studies have looked at how legislators' race affects how well they represent African American constituents (e.g., Lublin 1997; Canon 1999; Tate 2003) or how the concentration of minorities in electoral districts shapes various electoral and policy outcomes (e.g., Guinier 1994; Radcliff and Saiz 1995; Cameron, Epstein, and O'Halloran 1996; Lublin 1997; Whitby 1997; Canon 1999). As Griffin and Newman put it, "[T]hese studies essentially examine the circumstances under which racial or ethnic minorities are better, rather than equally, represented" (2007, 1033; see also Verba 2003). The constituency service field experiments allow me to measure whether different groups are equally treated because the outcome measure is directly comparable across groups.

Third, studying how responsive public officials are to constituency communications is also important because it examines a crucial means by which citizens access government resources. Elected officials and their staffs often help citizens navigate the federal and state bureaucracy to receive government help. Such constituent requests are an important way in which citizens gain access to government resources (Eulau and Karps 1977; Fiorina 1989).

Citizens recognize the importance of such constituency service and believe it is an important part of public officials' duties. Indeed, Harden (2013) found that voters think helping constituents with their service requests is as important as "learning about constituents' opinions in order to better represent their views."

Evidence shows that citizens avail themselves of their elected officials' help. Surveys conducted by the Congressional Management Foundation found that contacting one's representatives in Congress is one of the most common civic activities that citizens engage in. Nearly half of those surveyed reported contacting one of their MCs in the past five years. In contrast, less than 20 percent of respondents reported attending a political protest, speech, or rally. Citizens were also more likely to have contacted one of their congressional representatives than they were to have joined an interest group, volunteered, or given money to a political or advocacy campaign.

The degree to which public officials provide service to their constituents in turn affects the constituents' levels of political efficacy and engagement. Evidence suggests that when minorities and women view their representatives as more responsive, they participate in politics at higher rates (Chattopadhyay and Duflo 2004; Griffin and Keane 2006; Barreto 2007, 2010; cf. Lawless 2004; Dolan 2006). Consequently, studying public officials' responsiveness provides information about the likely effect of descriptive representation on voters' political efficacy and participation. Not surprisingly, Fiorina (1989) listed casework as one of lawmakers' three main duties along with lawmaking and pork-barreling. Given how little we know about this behavior, it is worth studying these activities in their own right.

Do Representatives Act as if Responsive Service Is One of Their Duties?

The first study I present was designed to discover whether legislators *act* as if constituency service is one of their duties. Although there are strong reasons to classify and study casework as an important part of elected officials' duties (see the preceding discussion), we do not know whether they *act* as if it is. To test this proposition I ran a two-wave study using constituency service requests sent to legislators who were retiring and others who were not. If politicians view constituency service as one of their duties, they should become less responsive to these types of requests when they retire.

The logic for this test is derived from research looking at how retirement affects legislators' roll call behavior. Rothenberg and Sanders (2000) conducted a test on the effect of retirement by examining how MCs acted in the last six months of each Congress. The advantage of limiting the analysis to the last six months is that by this time the deadline to file for running for reelection has passed, meaning that members have generally decided at that point whether they intend to run again. In looking at the behavior of members during the last six months, Rothenberg and Sanders found that members are more likely to abstain on roll call votes if they are going to retire. Even though these members do not have the arduous duties associated with conducting a reelection campaign, they actually make less time to show up for roll call votes. Without the electoral motivation hanging over their heads, retiring lawmakers put less effort into their duties. Thus, if legislators also view constituency service as one of their duties, retiring legislators should also be less likely to respond to e-mails.

One difficulty in testing whether retirement affects legislators' behavior is that we cannot randomly assign the date when state legislators are going to retire. The inability to randomly assign the retirement decision affects our ability to interpret the results we find. For example, even if we find that legislators who retire provide less service, there are multiple ways to interpret that finding. It may be that the decision to retire caused these legislators to put less effort into helping constituents because they no longer viewed it as a duty. However, it may also be that the legislators who put less effort into their jobs are the ones who are most likely to retire, possibly because they are more likely to lose if they do not.

I use a two-wave study design and the natural variation that occurs in state legislatures with staggered elections to gain more confidence that I can identify the way legislators' retirement decisions affect their behavior. The first wave of the study came in September 2009, with the second wave following in September 2010. In both waves all legislators in the study received an e-mail requesting help. Questions were randomly drawn from the list of questions in the Chapter 3 Appendix. Further, eighty-two different aliases were used across the two waves,[4] with different legislators randomly assigned to receive e-mails from different aliases.

---

[4] The aliases were Abigail Haas, Allison Krueger, Amy Phillips, Anne Smith, Anthony Campbell, Barbara Wilson, Betty Green, Brian Mitchell, Carly Schroeder, Carol Phillips, Carrie Novak, Christopher Clark, Claire Smith, Cole Clark, Colin Adams, Daniel Walker, David Moore, Deborah Bailey, Donald Young, Donna Roberts, Dorothy Lee, Dustin Smith, Edward Nelson, Elizabeth Thomas, Emily Evans, Emma Mueller, Frank Cox, Garrett Miller, Gary Reed, Geoffrey Anderson, George Wright, Heather Haas, Helen Baker, Hunter Smith, Jack Nelson, Jacob Allen, James Smith, Jason Collins, Jay Martin, Jeffrey Cooper, Jennifer Taylor, Jessica

The timing of the two e-mails was chosen in order to observe how legislators behave at different points in their legislative service. At the time of the second e-mail, the legislators serving in seats not up for election (because their seats were not up until 2012) still had two more years of service. However, the legislators serving in the seats up for election were either retiring from the position or running for reelection. By comparing the cross-sectional variation at the time of the second e-mail we can see whether the behavior of legislators who are retiring is different from that of legislators who are still serving (and also those running for reelection). This comparison alone, however, is subject to bias from self-selection. Herein lies the advantage of conducting the early wave. When I sent the first e-mail in 2009, all the legislators had at least one more full year of service, and so retirement should not have affected their behavior at the time. Thus, if the retiring legislators provide less service in 2010 but are indistinguishable from their fellow legislators in 2009, we have greater confidence that the decision to retire is affecting their behavior (and that the results are not an artifact of selection). In other words, the 2009 wave serves as a placebo test, showing how all the legislators responded to the requests when they still had significant time left in their service.

The legislators I used in this study came from twenty-six state legislative chambers. In twenty-five U.S. states, the upper chamber has staggered elections,[5] and in one state, North Dakota, members in the lower chamber also have staggered elections. I sent two e-mails to all of the nearly one thousand legislators in these twenty-six chambers.

The results for the 2010 wave, presented in the top half of Table 3.1, show that retiring legislators were significantly less likely to respond to the e-mails they received. While legislators who were not up for election until 2012 responded to 58 percent of the e-mails they received, retiring legislators only responded to 31 percent – about half as often. Retiring legislators reduced the effort they put into this aspect of their work by half. In contrast, the difference between legislators who were running for reelection and those who were not up for reelection until 2012 was only three percentage points, and not statistically significant.

The results from the 2009 wave allow us to test whether this large difference between retiring legislators and everyone else is simply an artifact of selection.

Richardson, Jill Phillips, John Brown, Joseph Martin, Kaitlin King, Karen Hill, Kathryn Schneider, Kenneth Scott, Kevin Evans, Kim Bell, Larry Murphy, Laura Rogers, Linda Davis, Lisa Hall, Margaret Robinson, Maria White, Mark Allen, Mary Johnson, Matthew Martin, Matthew Morris, Michael Miller, Michelle Stewart, Nancy King, Patricia Jones, Paul Lewis, Richard Jackson, Robert Williams, Ronald Turner, Ruth Parker, Sandra Carter, Sarah Cook, Scott Schmidt, Scott Ward, Sharon Edwards, Shirley Howard, Steven Adams, Susan Thompson, Tanner Schwartz, Timothy Morgan, William Anderson, and Wyatt Clark.

5 These states are Alaska, Arkansas, California, Colorado, Delaware, Florida, Hawaii, Iowa, Illinois, Indiana, Missouri, Montana, North Dakota, Nebraska, Nevada, Ohio, Oklahoma, Oregon, Pennsylvania, Tennessee, Utah, Washington, Wisconsin, West Virginia, and Wyoming.

TABLE 3.1. *Election Timing and Responsiveness of Politicians with Staggered Elections*

(A) 2010 Wave

	Responded	Timely Response	Answered Question
No Election (until 2012)	58.0%	52.2%	52.1%
Up for Reelection	61.2%	56.3%	54.7%
Retiring from Office	30.6%	29.1%	27.2%
Difference: Retiring – No Election	−27.4**	−23.1**	−22.1**
(Std. Error)	(4.7)	(4.8)	(3.4)
Difference: Reelection – No Election	3.2	4.1	2.9
(Std. Error)	(3.4)	(3.4)	(3.4)

(B) 2009 Wave (Placebo Test)

	Responded	Timely Response	Answered Question
No Election (until 2012)	58.0%	50.0%	44.2%
Up for Reelection	61.8%	57.2%	48.9%
Retiring from Office	53.7%	49.3%	41.0%
Difference: Retiring – No Election	−4.3	−0.7	−3.2
(Std. Error)	(4.8)	(4.9)	(4.8)
Difference: Reelection – No Election	3.8	7.2*	4.7
(Std. Error)	(3.4)	(3.5)	(3.5)
Observations	982	982	982

Notes: **Sig at the 0.01 level (one-tailed), *Sig at the 0.05 level (one-tailed). The experiment included a total of 982 officials (No Election until 2012 N = 500; Up for Reelection N = 348; Retiring from Office N = 134). The percentages in the table give the percentage of legislators whose responses met the requirements for the measured outcome. The differences are reported at the bottom of each section with the standard errors given in parentheses.

As was outlined earlier, one concern is that this difference could arise if those legislators who chose to retire were simply the type of legislator who is less responsive generally. If the results were in fact a result of this selection process, we should be able to observe a difference in these legislators' behavior in 2009.

Significantly, the results from the 2009 e-mails suggest that selection is not driving them. There were no significant differences in the behavior of the legislators in 2009. Although the retiring legislators were four percentage points less responsive than those whose seats were not up for election until 2012, this difference is not statistically significant (and is much smaller than the twenty-seven-percentage-point effect in 2010). Further, the difference-in-differences estimate of twenty-three percentage points is statistically significant. Once legislators know that they are going to retire, they put less effort into their duties. Previous work has shown that retiring legislators are less likely to participate in roll call votes (Rothenberg and Sanders 2000); retiring legislators are also less likely to respond to e-mail requests. Officials act as though constituent communication is one of the duties associated with their office. We should expect them to be responsive to constituents' requests.

The Electoral Benefits of Responding to Constituent Service Requests

Another reason that elected officials may be highly responsive to the communications they receive is that they have electoral incentives to do so. Legislators are unlikely to offend constituents when responding to these requests, and thus lawmakers can win over many different types of constituents, including those opposed to them for either partisan or policy reasons, by assisting them with service-related problems or questions (see, e.g., Cover and Brumberg 1982; Serra and Cover 1992). Some legislators' responses explicitly connected the e-mails they received to their electoral interests. One legislator who received an e-mail asking for help in registering to vote provided this response.

Dear Mr. Jackson,

Due to election ethic laws, I am not able to assist you, but the appropriate person to contact would be your county clerk to find out more information to register. You can find the county clerk's contact information either by checking the government pages in your phone book, or by doing a quick search on the internet.

Again, sorry I cannot be of more help, but there are strict laws governing elected officials.

Sincerely,
[redacted]

This legislator clearly felt that helping this constituent fell under the purview of his or her reelection efforts. This reasoning is understandable given that the legislator was being asked for help in registering to vote. However, a staffer in another legislative office responded similarly when the putative constituent, who identified herself as copartisan with the legislator, asked the legislator for information about the do-not-call list.

Shanice:

This email address is used for State Business. Please send this message any politically related emails to Rep [redacted] personal email address at [redacted].

Thanks,
[redacted]
Chief of Staff

In other cases, the legislators simply asked for the putative constituent's vote (see the discussion in Chapter 5). Legislators see this type of service as a chance to win over voters, which is why service is considered one of legislators' most important reelection tools (Cain, Ferejohn, and Fiorina 1987; King 1991).

TABLE 3.2. *Satisfaction with House Member Contact and Their Job Approval Rating*

	Job Approval Rating for Representative in U.S. House			
Satisfaction with Contact	Strongly Approve	Somewhat Approve	Somewhat Disapprove	Strongly Disapprove
Very Satisfied	2,902 (63.7%)	1,448 (31.8%)	146 (3.2%)	63 (1.4%)
Somewhat Satisfied	538 (18.0%)	1,556 (52.1%)	596 (19.9%)	299 (10.0%)
Not Very Satisfied	45 (2.6%)	357 (20.4%)	601 (34.3%)	747 (42.7%)
Not at All Satisfied	10 (0.6%)	91 (5.7%)	255 (16.0%)	1,237 (77.7%)

Notes: Data taken from the 2008 CCES study (Ansolabehere 2009). Each cell gives the number of individuals in that category, and the row percentage is given in parentheses.

Evidence shows that politicians are correct to believe that constituency service provides important electoral benefits. Table 3.2 shows that citizens' satisfaction with the responses they receive from their MC strongly predicts how much they approve of their representative. The data in Table 3.2 come from the 2008 Cooperative Congressional Election Study (CCES) common content (Ansolabehere 2009) and is limited to respondents who said they or someone in their family had contacted their MC. Among citizens who reported being very satisfied with their MC's response, more than 60 percent strongly approved of the job their MC was doing. In contrast, among those who were not at all satisfied with the response they received, nearly 80 percent strongly disapproved of the job their MC was doing.

While these data show a strong relationship between satisfaction with one's MC and satisfaction with how responsive that member is to citizens' communications, this study cannot identify the causal direction of that relationship. Also, because the CCES did not ask whether citizens received a response, we do not know whether they were dissatisfied because they received a response they did not like or because they did not receive a response at all.

Chris Karpowitz, Jeremy Pope, and I were able to overcome these issues and corroborate the relationship (Butler, Karpowitz, and Pope 2011). In our study we surveyed participants about their attitudes toward their MCs before they sent letters to them and nine months later when some had received a response. Controlling for individuals' prior levels of approval, receiving a letter strongly affected how much participants approved of their MCs. Further, the more satisfied individuals were with the letter they received, the more they approved of the MC. Even people who reported not being at all satisfied with the response they received had higher approval ratings for their MCs than those who did not receive a response (although this difference was statistically insignificant). In other words, sending a response never hurts the legislator, even when the content is deemed unsatisfactory. Legislators should be as responsive as possible to the mail they receive: there seems to be no downside to responding and the potential for a significant upside if the recipient feels even somewhat satisfied with the response.

Because the constituency service experiments presented in this book all involve sending simple service requests that do not require legislators to send answers that would alienate the recipient, legislators have incentives to respond to all the requests they receive. These response incentives highlight the implications of finding any differential treatment. If legislators are willing to engage in differential treatment even when there are no strong reasons to expect it, this raises concerns that they may engage in differential treatment in the other duties they undertake.

Why Officials Might Not Respond to Every Letter and E-mail

Conventional wisdom, engendered by the legislators themselves, also suggests that elected officials respond to all the letters and e-mails they receive. Mo Udall, who served for a long time as a congressman from Arizona, wrote a well-known newsletter for his constituents on "The Right to Write: Some Suggestions on Writing Your Congressman" (1967). Congressman Udall worried that too few of his constituents were writing him letters because of misconceptions, including the idea that "congressmen have no time or inclination to read their mail, [and] that a letter probably won't be answered or answered satisfactorily." In response to these and other concerns, Udall raised a number of counterpoints. His first point was that he read every letter.

Let me say that I read every letter written me by a constituent; a staff member may process it initially, but it will be answered and I will insist on reading it and personally signing the reply. (Udall 1967)

With such declarations it is not surprising that legislators are expected to respond to everyone. However, there are three reasons to expect that this may no longer be the case (if it ever was).

First, legislators who claim to be hyperresponsive to their constituents are probably not representative of all legislators. Legislators in office want to convince voters that they are concerned about their interests. Those who ignore a large percentage of the letters they receive are unlikely to discuss constituent communication; they have no reason to advertise information that hurts the image they want to build. Even after legislators leave office, they typically want to be remembered positively and so are unlikely to discuss constituent communication in a memoir unless they were relatively responsive during their years of active public service. Compounding this selection concern is the possibility that social desirability bias causes legislators to misrepresent themselves as being more responsive to constituents than they truly are.

Second, the rise of permanent campaigning means that legislators are busier than they were in the late 1960s, when Udall reported reading and responding to every letter. Legislators now spend more time raising money and engaging in campaign activities (Blumenthal 1980; Ornstein and Mann 2000), meaning that they have less time to spend on legislative activities. Constituent communication may be reduced to make time for campaigning.

Third, legislators now have more communications to respond to. Between 1994 and 2005, the volume of mail and e-mail sent to Congress quadrupled (Fitch and Goldsmidt 2005), and congressional offices now receive hundreds of communications each day. My congresswoman at the time I write this – Rosa DeLauro – claims on her website that she receives an average of 500 letters, e-mails, faxes, or calls per day. Even if that only refers to the five-day workweek, it still amounts to roughly 2,500 such contacts per week. The most recent measure, taken in 2004, indicates that MCs receive over 200 million pieces of e-mail or mail each year (Fitch and Goldschmidt 2005), an average of nearly 374,000 per legislator each year.

There is every reason to expect that state legislators also receive more communications from their constituents than they used to. In the automatic responses that legislators sent in response to the e-mail requests in the constituency service field experiments, many state legislators discussed the large number of messages they receive. One legislator, from a state with fairly large districts, described receiving "thousands of e-mails each month." Another, in a state with moderately sized districts, cited the number of e-mails she received to explain why she did not always respond quickly.

Since I personally read and review each of the hundreds of e-mails I receive daily, it often takes time to respond to everyone.

The increase in the number of messages was large enough that one legislator created a second e-mail account, which only his constituents could use. Part of his automated response read:

For the constituents in my district, I have a special e-mail address for you only. You may call [redacted]. They will give you the e-mail address for my "special" constituents. I look forward to working with you.

Because legislators may exaggerate the number of constituent communications they receive, I view these numbers as an upper bar. However, it seems reasonable to assume that over time state legislators, like federal legislators, have received an increasing amount of mail and e-mail from their constituents. It takes time to respond to these requests, and with constrained resources legislators must choose which messages to respond to. The constituency service field experiments in Chapters 5 and 6 reveal some of the factors that affect legislators' decisions to respond.

Chapter 3 Appendix

Questions Used in the Constituency Service Studies

What follows is the list of questions used in the two rounds of the elections experiment (Chapter 3) and in the 2010 race/ethnicity study (Chapter 6). While the questions were drawn from several sources, many come from the websites of state legislators who were providing answers to questions they frequently receive. I tried to use the questions they were most frequently asked in order to increase the external validity of the experiments.

Q1: I was trying to figure out my latest paycheck and wanted to know what my employer can lawfully deduct from my wages. Do you know?

Thanks,

Q2: I'm wondering what I need to do to establish residency so that my son will be eligible for in-state tuition when he goes to college.

Sincerely,

Q3: I was trying to figure out the election calendar, do you know where I can find out when local elections are scheduled?

Q4: What steps do I take to be added to the do not call list?

Q5: I just barely started renting out my house and I wanted to know whether I needed to do anything at this point for tax purposes, or if I can just wait until I file next year.

Thanks,

Q6: I'm trying to figure out laws relating to breaks during work. If I'm a smoker, do I get additional rest breaks?

Best,

Q7: I heard about a cash for fridge program but I haven't been able to figure out how it works. Is there anywhere I can learn about the program?

Sincerely,

Q8: Do I need to apply to run a car wash if we are doing it to raise funds for a non-profit group?

Q9: If I break company property while performing my job, can my employer deduct the cost from my wages?

Best,

Q10: I haven't taken the time to switch to digital TV yet. Do you know if I can still do that without buying a new TV and what steps I should take?

Q11: Does the state list anywhere the jobs in state government? I'm interested in finding out what is available.

I appreciate your help,

Q12: At one point it seemed like there were lots of programs to help give people incentives to buy homes. I'm renting now but would consider buying a home. Does the state have any programs or incentives to buy a home?

Sincerely,

Q13: I'm wondering how long we need to live here before members of my family become eligible for in-state tuition.

Thanks for your help,

Q14: I can't seem to find my child's birth certificate. Do you know who I can contact in order to get another copy?

Thanks,

Q15: What are the laws about getting breaks for breastfeeding at work? Do women get breaks to do so?

Q16: Do you know whether I can register to vote when I apply for a driver's license?

Best,

Q17: I just sold my home and am wondering how I report the sale of a home on my taxes. Do I have to do anything at this point about that?

Q18: I was curious about learning about where different candidates get their money. Do you know if that information is public and how I can access it?

Thanks,

Q19: I heard about a program where the government will help pay something for new fridges. Will this be like the cash-for-clunkers program where I have to trade in my old fridge, or can I keep my old fridge?

Q20: I know that schools now have students take tests for the no child left behind program. Is there any way that I can find out the test scores for different schools in the state under that program?

Thanks,

Q21: I am wondering whether I need to bring some type of identification when I vote. Since I haven't registered to vote yet, this isn't a pressing matter, but I still thought it would be good to know.

Thanks,

Q22: I recently moved and am wondering how long I need to live here, before I can register to vote. Do you know?

Thank you,

Q23: I'm trying to learn about zoning laws and was wondering whether that is something that the state or the city is in charge of. If it is a state matter, who should I contact to learn what the zoning laws are?

Best,

Q24: When the legislature is in session, are citizens allowed to come and watch the discussion? If so, how can I find out what the legislators will be discussing?

Thank you for your help,

Q25: I have a child who will be starting school soon and I'm wondering what I need to do to enroll them. Thanks for any help you can provide.

Q26: Given how bad the economy seems to be I'm planning on starting a side business. Can you tell me where I can learn more about applying for a business license?

Sincerely,

Q27: I just moved here from out of state and was wondering what the laws are regarding smoking in public areas.

Thanks,

Q28: With the budget cuts I've been reading about a lot of states taking furloughs. Are any of our state officials taking furloughs? If so, which departments will it affect and on what days? Can I still go to the DMV anytime I want?

Best,

Q29: What steps do I need to take if I want to vote absentee in the next election?

Thanks,

Q30: If I ever want to make a complaint about a telemarketing call, who should I contact?

Thank you for your help,

Q31: I have children in school and I want to know how my school compares with others in the state. Do you know whether I can get that type of information somewhere?

Thanks,

Q32: I realize that the election is still a ways off, but I'm still wondering about whether there is a deadline to register to vote.

Best,

Q33: I'm on the do not call list but got called to take a survey. Do you know if that's legal? Sorry, I know it's a simple question, but sometimes I get sick of getting so many phone calls at night.

Thanks,

Q34: I wanted to buy a new car and was wondering whether the program for getting a new car with good gas mileage is still in place. Also is the state giving any incentives to buy new cars?

Thanks,

Q35: My child will start school next year and I'm trying to remember what immunizations they need. Do you know that information or where I might find it?

Thanks,

Q36: We just moved into the area and I'm trying to figure out how to find my polling place. Is there a site that lists the location of polling places?

Sincerely,

Q37: I was wondering whether there is a website that keeps track of which firms win state contracts for various construction projects?

Q38: I'm just trying to figure out which legislative district I live in. Is there a website somewhere that I can easily do that?

Thanks,

Q39: I'm thinking about starting a new company and want to be sure that I get any licensing that I need. Who do I contact about that?

Q40: If I feel strongly about an issue, is there any way to let my voice be heard. Does the legislature have open town hall meetings or some other mechanism for citizens to express their opinions.

Thanks,

4

Bias in the Way Officials Process Constituents' Opinions

Imagine yourself as an elected official in a city that is considering the issue of school vouchers. As part of that debate you receive the following letter advocating for the use of vouchers.

Dear Mayor,

I have lived in the community for about 10 years, working as an attorney. I am writing to ask that you support any attempt to move to a school vouchers system. Vouchers would improve the quality of education in our schools system.

 Thank you for your consideration,

Best regards,
Ron Smith

Do you think the person who wrote this letter understands the complexities of the issues surrounding the use of school vouchers? Do you think the person who wrote this letter holds his position strongly? Would your answers to these questions change if the writer had been a janitor instead of an attorney?

 Elected officials gather information about their constituents' opinions and preferences during visits to their district, through opinion polls, and through the letters they receive. As officials gather this information they must decide how to weigh different constituents' opinions. If officials feel that some groups' opinions are less likely to be based on thorough research and/or do not represent deeply held convictions, these groups will have less influence on elected officials' actions.

Rationalizing the Decision to Discount Some Constituents' Preferences

In this chapter I test whether public officials use either or both of two potential rationalizations that would lead them to discount the opinions of some constituents. Because the use of one of these rationalizations does not necessitate or preclude the use of the other, I test whether elected officials are using either, or possibly even both. These potential rationalizations emerge from the process by which elected officials reach decisions on how to vote.[1] Because legislators take many factors into account when reaching decisions (see Kingdon 1981; Butler and Nickerson 2011), there are several opportunities for elected officials to discount constituents' preferences.

One way in which elected officials can rationalize putting less weight on some constituents' opinions is by assuming that some constituents care less about the issue than others do. If constituents care less about the issue, they are less likely to know what action the public official takes and are less likely to hold that official accountable for it (Converse 1964; Krosnick 1990; Iyengar et al. 2008). Previous studies conclude that politicians respond to these incentives and are in fact less responsive to the preferences of constituents who feel less strongly about an issue (e.g., Kingdon 1981; Wlezien 2004). Because politicians are more responsive to constituents with intense preferences, they can justify ignoring the wishes of constituents whose preferences (they think) are less intense.

I also test for a second type of rationalization: that some constituents understand less about the issue than others do. Evidence shows that voters who are more confident about an issue are more willing to punish politicians who are out of step on that issue (Gerber et al. 2011). Politicians thus might expect less retribution from voters who they think are less informed about the topic.

Further, legislators may believe that they can change the opinions of constituents who know less about the matter in question (Fenno 1978; Jacobs and Shapiro 2000; Gabel and Scheve 2007). If elected officials think constituents are misinformed, they may believe that these constituents are likely to come around to their way of thinking when they learn more about the issue.

These are not the only ways in which public officials might rationalize discounting the opinions of their constituents. In that sense, the results here may be the lower bar in terms of the bias that public officials exhibit because the bias may be compounded with other potential avenues for discounting voters' preferences.

In sum, I test whether public officials use either of two potential rationalizations that would lead them to discount the opinions of some constituents. First, public officials might assume that some constituents care less about the issue. Second, public officials might assume that constituents with different opinions are less informed about the topic. In what follows, I present several

---

[1] There are other ways in which public officials might rationalize ignoring constituents' opinions. I chose to focus on the role of these two rationalizations because research on the behavior of public officials suggests that these are important considerations they take into account. These experiments thus test for the very bias that would affect political outcomes because it affects the considerations that politicians use.

We are trying to learn about how municipal officials make decisions by giving you a number of scenarios and asking how you would act in each instance. We have intentionally kept these scenarios short, and focused on key elements in order to not take up much of your time.

Scenario 1: A municipal official received the following email.

Ron Smith
to me ▾

Dear ███████████.

I have lived in the community for about 10 years, working as an attorney. I am writing to ask that you support any attempt to move to a school vouchers system. Vouchers would improve the quality of education in our schools system.

Thank you for your consideration,

Best regards,
Ron Smith

Please indicate whether you agree or disagree with each of the following statements about this message?

	Agree	Disagree
This letter was likely a form letter sent by an interest group	○	○
The writer likely understands the complexities of this issue	○	○
The writer likely holds this position strongly	○	○
The writer likely based his opinions on facts	○	○

FIGURE 4.1. Constituents' socioeconomic status and legislators' perceptions of their letters: text of the survey experiment. This provides a screen shot of what city officials taking the survey would have seen. The profession of the person sending the e-mail was varied across the treatments (attorney versus janitor).

experiments designed to test whether constituents' race, gender, and/or SES predicts public officials' willingness to express either, or both, of these rationales when evaluating a hypothetical constituent's opinions.

Survey Experiments Testing for Bias When Evaluating Constituents' Opinions

In August 2012, I conducted a survey of city officials wherein I implemented the thought experiment presented at the beginning of this chapter. Half of the officials taking the survey were shown the letter from the attorney to the mayor, displayed as a JPEG file that looked like a screen shot of an actual e-mail (see Figure 4.1), and the other half a letter written by an "office park janitor."[2]

I conducted similar survey experiments on city and state officials to test for bias based on the constituent's gender and also his or her race or ethnicity. I

---

[2] I also randomized whether the letter supported or opposed school vouchers. The results of randomizing the position of the letter writer show that public officials exhibit a bias in which they rate the opinions of writers who agree with them as being more thoughtful (Butler 2013).

designed these experiments to test whether elected officials feel that some types of constituents have more intense preferences and/or more thoughtful opinions.

The survey experiments on city officials were part of the 2012 American Municipal Officials Survey that Adam Dynes and I conducted. We emailed city officials from across the United States an invitation and link to take the survey. The response rate was 20 percent, with officials from larger towns and cities being slightly more likely to take the survey. More details about the survey are given in the Chapter 4 Appendix.

Municipal Officials' Perceptions by Constituents' Socioeconomic Status

I used the experiment introduced at the beginning of this chapter to test whether municipal officials exhibit a bias against individuals with lower socioeconomic status. Figure 4.1 shows the screen shot of the question officials received from the attorney supporting school vouchers. The screen shot was used in order to increase the realism of the scenario.

I kept the length of the e-mail short for two reasons. First, I wanted to keep the survey short in order to minimize the strain on public officials' time. Second, and more important, I wanted to gauge politicians' reactions to the SES of the writer. The e-mail is short and straightforward. The reaction of the respondents is attributable to the profession of the writer and not to something about the language of the text.

The key feature of the experiment is that municipal officials in this scenario were shown an identical letter from either an attorney or an office park janitor.[3] I chose these professions because individuals are familiar with them and view attorneys as having high socioeconomic status and janitors as having low status. I chose to emphasize that the janitor was connected with an office park in order to signal that he did not work at a school. I did not want the lower socioeconomic treatment to be conflated with the possibility that the letter writer had a vested economic interest in the outcome because he was a janitor for the school district.

I conducted this experiment to test whether public officials were more likely to rationalize that a low-SES constituent's opinion should be discounted more than a high-SES constituent's opinion. As I discussed earlier, there are at least two ways in which officials might rationalize discounting someone's opinion: they might assume that the constituent's position is not well thought out and/or that it is an issue that the constituent does not feel strongly about.[4]

---

[3] The main body of the e-mail was manipulated in the following ways in order to signal the treatments: "I have lived in the community for about 10 years, working as an [attorney/office park janitor]. I am writing to ask that you [support/oppose] any attempt to move to a school vouchers system. Vouchers would [improve/hurt] the quality of education in our schools system."

[4] A third possibility is that they might conclude that the opinion is not representative of those of the other voters in the district. I do not test for this possibility because it is likely to be a function of how active a given group is in actually contacting the official (Verba 2003) and so

I measured whether the public officials thought the letter was well thought out and represented a strong position by asking respondents to agree or disagree with the following statements after they read the e-mail.

> This letter was likely a form letter sent by an interest group.
> The writer likely holds this position strongly.
> The writer likely understands the complexities of this issue.
> The writer likely based his opinions on facts.

In addition to directly asking elected officials whether the *writer likely holds this position strongly*, I asked the officials to rate whether *this letter was likely a form letter*. Surveys show that the two most common reasons that citizens contact their U.S. senator or representative are that they care deeply about the issue and/or they were asked to do so by an organization they trust (Goldschmidt and Ochreiter, 2008). Public officials may be more likely to discount form letters by rationalizing that the constituent only sent the letter because he was asked to do so (not because he personally felt strongly about the issue).

I asked about agreement with the other two statements – *the writer likely understands the complexities of this issue* and *the writer likely based his opinions on facts* – in order to test for the second possible rationalization. Understanding the complexities of an issue and basing one's opinion on facts means that the constituent likely has done more to investigate the issue. The reverse is also true. Constituents who are less understanding of an issue and do not understand the facts have probably put less research into the issue. These are also the type of constituents to whom elected officials may believe they should be less responsive because they are unlikely to hold politicians accountable or because politicians feel they can influence their opinions on the issue. For the analysis, I present the percentage that agreed with each statement by the SES treatment (attorney versus janitor).

In addition to testing public officials' overall response to constituents' SES, I also present the results by the public official's income. In designing the experiment, my expectation was that lower-income public officials would be less likely to discount the janitor's opinion than their higher-income counterparts would. The officials' own income status was based on a question posed earlier in the same survey, which asked about their families' annual income in the previous year. I present the results separately by whether the respondent made more or less than fifty-five thousand dollars in the previous year.[5]

Table 4.1 presents the results for how public officials responded to the attorney versus janitor treatments. The top half of the table presents the results

---

depends heavily on voters' actions. In contrast, we can directly measure whether the demographic characteristics of a letter writer leads public officials to discount the writer's opinion.

[5] The approximately ninety individuals who chose not to state their income are excluded from this part of the analysis.

TABLE 4.1. *Do Officials Exhibit Socioeconomic Bias at the Input Stage of Representation?*

	Form Letter	Strong Position	Understand	Fact-Based
Attorney	52.3%	67.9%	34.2%	28.6%
Janitor	53.5%	62.9%	20.2%	20.1%
Difference	−1.2	5.0	14.0**	8.5**
	(3.7)	(3.5)	(3.3)	(3.2)
Obs.	724	719	702	696

	Form Letter		Strong Position		Understand		Fact-based	
Income:	<$55K	>$55K	<$55K	>$55K	<$55K	>$55K	<$55K	>$55K
Attorney	48.0%	52.0%	81.6%	67.6%	42.5%	32.8%	46.8%	28.2%
Janitor	68.4%	48.8%	62.5%	65.0%	23.2%	18.1%	19.6%	19.6%
Difference	−20.4*	3.2	19.1*	2.6	19.3*	14.7**	27.2**	8.6*
	(9.4)	(4.4)	(8.7)	(4.1)	(9.1)	(3.8)	(8.9)	(3.8)
Obs.	107	525	105	522	103	510	103	504

Notes: Standard errors are given in parentheses. **Sig at the 0.01 level (one-tailed), * Sig at the 0.05 level (one-tailed). K = thousands.

for the full sample. About half of the respondents in the experiment thought the letter was a form letter. This was true for respondents who saw the letter from the attorney as well as those who saw the letter from the janitor. For this outcome city officials did not rate the letters from janitors differently than the letters from attorneys. There is some weak evidence that the writer's profession affected respondents' ratings of the strength of the writer's position. Respondents who read the letter from the attorney were five percentage points more likely to agree that the letter writer held the position strongly; however, this difference is not statistically significant.

The elected officials did, however, think that the attorney was more likely to know about the issues. Respondents were eight percentage points more likely to think that the letter writer based his opinion on facts if the attorney had written the letter (a statistically significant difference). Similarly, city officials thought that the attorney was much more likely to understand the complexities of the issue. Only 20 percent of officials thought the janitor understood the complexities of the issue, but 34 percent thought the attorney understood the complexities of the issue. This fourteen-percentage-point difference is large and statistically significant.

The advantage of conducting the experiment is that we are able to attribute the large difference in how public officials responded to the letter writer's occupation rather than the content of the letter. In practice, lower-income individuals may use different language when contacting their elected officials. They may in fact use weaker arguments or do other things that could possibly explain why public officials are more dismissive of their opinions. Because of my experimental design, those concerns cannot explain the results. The content of the e-mail is simple, straightforward, and held constant across treatments.

When low-SES and high-SES individuals send the same letters, elected officials are much more dismissive of the low-SES individuals' opinions because they have a lower SES.

Public officials' dismissive attitude toward low-SES individuals means that previous studies have underestimated the bias these constituents face. Previous results have focused on the advantages that high-SES individuals enjoy in terms of greater resources and the kind of connections that make it easier to politically participate at a higher rate (Verba, Schlozman, and Brady 1995; Verba 2003). These results show that the differences in resources for political participation can only be part of the story. Even when low-SES individuals participate at the same rate as high-SES individuals do, officials take the input from high-SES individuals more seriously.

Low-SES individuals may in fact choose to participate less because they expect to see little payoff from becoming involved. Previous studies have shown that low-SES individuals feel that government officials are less likely to listen to people like them (e.g., Verba, Schlozman, and Brady 1995, 349), and this political efficacy deficit is cited as one reason that low-SES individuals participate less in politics. I have shown that these expectations may be rational. Elected officials assume that low-SES individuals are less likely to understand an issue's complexity and less likely to base their opinions on facts.

Would Increased Levels of Descriptive Representation Mitigate This Bias?

One reason we may see public officials discounting the opinions expressed by low-SES individuals is that city officials themselves are disproportionately middle- and upper-income individuals (Carnes 2012). The lack of descriptive representation may hurt low-income individuals. I evaluate this possibility by breaking the results down by whether the individual's annual income in the previous year was less or more than fifty-five thousand dollars (see the bottom portion of Table 4.1).

The results on descriptive representation are surprising because low-income officials exhibit greater levels of socioeconomic bias against low-SES individuals. When I designed the experiment I expected to find that low-income officials would rate the opinions of a low-SES individual more favorably. To the contrary, the results show that low-income officials are not more favorably disposed toward low-SES individuals. In fact, low-income officials are twenty percentage points more likely to think that a janitor would send a form letter. They are also significantly more likely to think that an attorney feels strongly about his or her position. Only 62 percent of low-income officials agreed that the janitor expressed a strongly held position, but 81 percent thought the attorney expressed a strongly held position.

By contrast, high-income officials do not discount constituents' intensity about an issue. High-income officials are not more likely to think that the janitor sent a form letter, and they believe that a janitor and an attorney are equally likely to feel strongly about an issue.

Although high-income officials do not seem to discount the intensity with which low-SES individuals hold a position, they do exhibit a socioeconomic bias when deciding whether the position is well thought out. High-income officials were about fifteen percentage points more likely to think an attorney understood the complexities of the issue than was a janitor. Similarly, they were about nine percentage points more likely to think that the attorney based his opinion on facts.

Again, however, the low-SES individuals exhibited an even larger bias. While 46 percent of the low-income individuals thought the attorney based his opinion on facts, less than 20 percent thought the janitor did. That twenty-seven-percentage-point difference means that the low-income individuals were more than twice as likely to think that the attorney was basing his opinion on facts. Similarly, the low-income officials exhibited a stronger bias than their high-income counterparts in terms of the writer's understanding of the issue (a difference of nineteen versus fifteen percentage points).

It is difficult to say why low-income individuals exhibit a greater socioeconomic bias than their high-income counterparts do. One tentative possibility is that low-income individuals put high-SES individuals on a pedestal. The results in Table 4.1 show that for the outcomes *strong position* and *fact-based* the low-income and high-income individuals rate the letters from the janitor to be about the same, but that the low-income individuals rate the attorney's position as being much more thoughtful and strong.

Whatever the cause of the higher levels of socioeconomic bias among low-income individuals, their consequence is the same: in this case, increased levels of descriptive representation do not lead to better representation of low-SES individuals. There may be other reasons to prefer greater representation for low-SES individuals (see Chapter 5), but decreasing the socioeconomic bias in the way officials process constituents' policy input is not one of them.

City Officials' Perceptions by Constituents' Gender

I conducted a second experiment to measure whether city officials exhibit any gender bias in response to constituents' positions with a different, randomly chosen subset of officials who participated in the 2012 American Municipal Officials Survey (see the Chapter 4 appendix for details on the survey). The question design is similar to that presented in Figure 4.1. The introduction to the question was the same, the follow-up questions were the same, and the e-mail itself was a picture taken from an actual message with the name of the recipient blacked out. The text of the e-mail is given in Box 4.1 (with the randomized parts in bold and italic type).

A key aspect of the experiment is that I randomized the name of the constituent who sent the letter. There were a total of four names: two women

---

BOX 4.1. **Text of the E-mail in the Gender Experiment**

Dear Mayor Henderson,

[I am writing to ask that you support efforts to consolidate 911 services with the neighboring areas. The quality of services will remain high and the long-term savings outweigh the start-up costs. /
I am writing to ask that you oppose efforts to consolidate 911 services with the neighboring areas. The quality of services will suffer and the start-up costs outweigh any long-term savings. /
Please support efforts that try to cut property taxes. The economy is not doing well and we cannot afford to tax citizens if we want the city to recover. We do not need many of the programs that the city pays for and therefore can change how we tax in this city. /
Please oppose efforts that try to cut property taxes. The economy is not doing well and we cannot afford to get in debt if we want the city to recover. We need the programs that the city pays for and therefore cannot change how we tax in this city.]

Sincerely,
[Joshua Wood/Melissa Wood/Eric Bennett/Amy Bennett]

Notes: The full text of the experiment on how officials responded to constituents' gender followed that of the experiment on constituents' SES (see Figure 4.1). This figure simply gives the text of the e-mail that participating officials were shown in that experiment (the e-mail itself was presented as a screen shot of an actual e-mail; again, see Figure 4.1). In the experiment the items in bold were randomly manipulated across treatments.

(Melissa Wood and Amy Bennett) and two men (Joshua Wood and Eric Bennett). I also chose to use the same last names for the women and men in order to preclude the possibility that respondents' reactions to the last names might drive any differences in how the men and women were treated. The randomized name appeared both at the end of each letter and at the top of the e-mail (see Figure 4.1 for the general layout of the e-mail and question).

Again, I asked public officials to agree or disagree with the following statements about the e-mail they read.

This letter was likely a form letter sent by an interest group.
The writer likely holds this position strongly.
The writer likely understands the complexities of this issue.
The writer likely based his or her opinions on facts.

The top part of Table 4.2 presents the percentage of people who agreed with each statement by the gender of the e-mail writer. Again, we see that most officials thought the e-mail was a form letter. Officials thought that about 63 percent of the letters from women and 58 percent of the letters from men were form letters. The difference does show that officials were about five percentage

TABLE 4.2. *Do Officials Exhibit Gender Bias at the Input Stage of Representation?*

	Form Letter	Strong Position	Understand	Fact-Based
Sample: All Municipal Officials				
Female	62.8%	67.0%	27.4%	27.9%
Male	58.2%	65.3%	26.2%	30.5%
Difference	4.6	1.7	1.2	−2.6
	(3.4)	(3.3)	(3.1)	(3.2)
Obs.	828	831	824	816
Sample: Only Male Municipal Officials				
Female	63.3%	66.8%	28.3%	29.6%
Male	60.1%	64.4%	24.3%	29.1%
Difference	3.2	2.4	4.0	0.5
	(3.9)	(3.8)	(3.5)	(3.7)
Obs.	631	631	625	620

Notes: Standard errors are given in parentheses. **Sig at the 0.01 level (one-tailed). *Sig at the 0.05 level (one-tailed).

points more likely to rate letters from women as being form letters. By itself this is some weak evidence that there might be a gender bias; however, when taken with the other evidence, the results are not supportive of the idea that there is a gender bias. The difference observed with the form letter does not reach levels of statistical significance, and all the other outcomes are even smaller in magnitude. Further, the results often point in the opposite direction. The public officials were nearly two percentage points more likely to think that women felt more strongly about the issue and one percentage point more likely to think that they understood the complexities of the issue better. Overall the results show a lack of gender-related bias.

We can also rule out the possibility that we are missing gender-related bias because male and female officials were exhibiting bias in opposite directions. If male and female officials were simply exhibiting a bias for their in-group, these biases could cancel each other out and make things appear unbiased on average. The bottom half of Table 4.2, however, looks at the behavior of the male public officials in the sample and shows that the results are nearly identical. Male officials are no more likely to think that men hold their positions strongly or better understand the issue. For each of the four outcomes, the differences are small and statistically insignificant. There is no evidence of a gender bias in the way elected officials' process constituents' opinions.

The lack of gender bias is also consistent with the findings of a recent study that looks at how well different constituents' preferences predict roll call votes (Griffin, Newman, and Wolbrecht 2012). The authors of that study find that both men's opinions and women's opinions are equally predictive of how legislators vote on roll calls. At the same time, other studies using a similar methodology find that public officials are much less responsive to the opinions of low-income constituents (Bartels 2008). I find the same pattern. Public officials evaluating constituents' opinions exhibit a marked socioeconomic bias but no gender bias.

State Legislators' Perceptions by Constituents' Race/Ethnicity

I also conducted a similar survey experiment on whether public officials discount constituents' opinions based on the race of the letter writer. In contrast to the other experiments, which were conducted with city officials, this last experiment was conducted with a sample of state legislators. The experiment on state legislators was part of a survey that was conducted in March 2012 and e-mailed to all of the roughly seven thousand state legislators in the United States. To account for the possibility that some staff members would fill out the survey on the legislator's behalf, the first question on the survey asked respondents whether they were a state legislator or a staff member. I present all the results with the self-identified state legislator subsample. Additional details about the survey itself are presented in the Chapter 4 Appendix.

In administering the survey, my co-investigators and I tried to keep it under five minutes because of concerns about burdening state legislators.[6] To keep the survey within the short time frame, some of the longer questions (including the survey experiment discussed here) were presented to only a subset of the subjects. This particular survey experiment was presented to only about six hundred respondents.[7]

The text of the experiment itself is similar to the survey experiments with city officials and is given in Box 4.2. In this case the respondents received an e-mail in which the writer asked the legislator to either oppose or support efforts to cut taxes.[8] I chose to focus on taxes versus spending cuts because this is an important issue that has been salient for decades. The key aspect of the experiment is that legislators were shown an e-mail from a constituent named James Smith, Javier Rodriguez, or LaShawn Washington as a signal for the constituents' putative race/ethnicity.

One difference between the survey experiment on state legislators (see Box 4.2) and those on city officials (see Figure 4.1) is that I did not ask the state legislators to rate whether they thought the letter writer based his opinion on facts. The survey of state legislators was conducted several months before

---

[6] Like response rates in the general population, response rates of congressional candidates have declined precipitously in recent years. One of the legislators who was invited to take the survey explained that he could not do so because he'd "gotten 5 similar requests this week." Given the small population of legislators, we were very conscious of keeping the survey short.

[7] The overall response rate for the survey was about 15 percent.

[8] The results of that experiment are described in Butler (2013) and show that public officials rate the constituents who agree with them as having a better understanding of the facts and, to a lesser extent, a stronger attachment to their position.

BOX 4.2. **Text of the Legislative Survey Experiment on Race**

We'll start with 5 scenarios involving 5 different legislators. Tell us how you think each legislator would act.

Scenario #_: A legislator receives the following email:

"Dear Representative [Redacted],

Please [**oppose/support**] legislation that tries to cut taxes. The economy is not doing well and we cannot afford to [**get in debt/tax citizens**] if we want the state to recover. We [**need/do not need many of**] the programs that the state pays for and therefore [**cannot/can**] change how we tax in this state.

Sincerely,
[**James Smith/Javier Rodriguez/LaShawn Washington**]"

How likely are the following statements to apply to this message? (Answer options: Likely, Unlikely)
   This was a form letter from an interest group
   The writer understands the complexities of this issue
   The writer holds this position strongly

Notes: This provides the full text of the e-mail that state legislators were shown. In the experiment the items in bold were randomly manipulated across treatments.

---

the survey of municipal officials. I added the fourth statement to provide a second measure of whether policymakers rationalize that some constituents do not understand the issue. Here are the three statements about the letter that the state legislators were asked to rate.

   This letter was likely a form letter sent by an interest group
   The writer likely holds this position strongly
   The writer likely understands the complexities of this issue

For the analysis, I present the percentage of legislators who agreed with each of these statements by the race/ethnicity of the letter writer.

The top half of Table 4.3 presents the results of the race experiment for all the state legislators in the sample. As before, the majority of elected officials say that the letter is likely a form letter and the writer probably does not understand much about the issue. However, unlike the study that looked at SES, elected officials do not discriminate against minorities. While legislators believe that only 18 percent of black constituents and 19 percent of Latino constituents understand the issue (based on this letter), these percentages are actually larger than the number of legislators who thought the white constituent understood the issue (only 15 percent thought whites understood the issue). Minority opinion is not discounted. If anything, the opinions of minorities are given slightly more credence than those of their white counterparts. In actuality,

TABLE 4.3. *Do Officials Exhibit Racial or Ethnic Bias at the Input Stage of Representation?*

	Form Letter	Strong Position	Understand
Sample: All Legislators			
Black constituent	66.7%	64.9%	18.0%
Latino constituent	72.9%	63.6%	19.2%
White constituent	68.6%	63.6%	15.3%
Difference: black – white	−1.9	1.3	2.7
	(4.7)	(5.0)	(3.9)
Difference: Latino – white	4.3	0.0	4.0
	(4.8)	(5.0)	(3.9)
Obs.	592	587	584
Sample: White Legislators Only			
Black constituent	68.8%	65.0%	16.9%
Latino constituent	72.3%	65.6%	20.7%
White constituent	67.5%	63.2%	15.8%
Difference: black – white	1.2	1.8	1.1
	(4.9)	(5.1)	(4.0)
Difference: Latino – white	4.7	2.4	4.9
	(5.0)	(5.1)	(4.1)
Obs.	555	552	549

Notes: Standard errors are given in parentheses. **Sig at the 0.01 level (one-tailed). *Sig at the 0.05 level (one-tailed).

of course, the results are not large (and are not statistically significant), and they even go in the unexpected direction.

The same pattern of racial equality characterizes the other outcomes. Race does not predict legislators' ratings of the strength of the writer's position or the likelihood that the e-mail was a form letter. For both outcomes the results indicate that blacks, whites, and Latinos are treated equally. Legislators were not engaging in racial or ethnic bias when reading these letters. They believed that black, white, and Latino constituents were equally likely to hold strong opinions and they did not think that one group understood the complexities of the issue better than another.

The results in the top half of Table 4.3 use the full sample of legislators – both minorities and whites. One possibility is that both groups are exhibiting bias in favor of constituents from their in-group, with the biases balancing each other out. In other words, it might be that there is a bias but we missed it by looking at all the legislators together.

The bottom half of Table 4.3 presents the results when the sample is limited to white legislators only. The results show that white legislators do not exhibit a bias against minority constituents. The differences largely work in the opposite direction. For example, the legislators are more likely to say that minorities feel strongly about the issue and understand the issue better than white constituents do. These differences are small and statistically insignificant, but it is noteworthy that they do not even go in the direction that would suggest there is a bias against racial minorities. It is not surprising that this is the same result we find with the full sample: the majority of legislators in the sample are white. Still, the main results are clear: legislators are not engaging in racial or ethnic bias when evaluating constituents' opinions.

Discussion

Political scientists have long thought about whose preferences are represented in democratic societies. Writing in the 1950s and 1960s, Robert Dahl (1967) and other political theorists argued for the idea of pluralism. In a pluralistic society there would not be one center of power, but multiple centers. Pluralism "sees the political system as reasonably open to multiple interests if these interests feel strongly enough about an issue to mobilize pressure" (Manley 1983, 369). In other words, those who feel more strongly about policy in a given area will determine policy in that area. In practice pluralists thought that groups would mobilize and advocate for the interests of voters who felt strongly about the issue.

Schattschneider (1960) attacked the pluralists' vision of a democratic society by noting that interest groups are not representative of American society. Drawing on several previous studies, Schattschneider highlighted that high-SES individuals were much more likely to participate in voluntary organizations. If interest groups were the key to representation in a pluralistic society, then such a society would be biased toward those who dominate such groups: the wealthy. As Schattschneider memorably put it, "The flaw in the pluralist heaven is that the heavenly chorus sings with a strong upper-class accent" (34–35).

The results here suggest that Schattschneider's critique might actually underestimate the socioeconomic bias in a pluralist system. Schattschneider's critique focused on differences in participation, suggesting that low-income constituents would be less well represented because they participated less in groups that would advocate for their interests. The experiments in this chapter show that even if they did participate at levels equal to those of high-SES constituents, their opinions would be discounted. Given similar levels of participation (e.g., sending the same letter), public officials assume that low-SES individuals are less thoughtful in forming their opinions.

The discounting of low-income constituents' opinions in this experiment is particularly disconcerting because the e-mails are simple, straightforward, and *constant*. This is important because in practice the janitor and attorney might use different language or arguments to express their opinions. In the experiment the letter from the attorney did not provide better arguments; the letters were the same. In the real world we might observe differences in how much these two groups participate and spend in elections or even differences in the level of thought behind the arguments the two groups make. It is possible that individuals from different backgrounds are in fact more informed than others.

However, that does not explain the bias in this experiment. The only difference here is the writer's job description: janitor versus lawyer. This study thus sets a baseline for the bias we would observe if there were no other differences. In other words, the results show how much bias individuals in low-SES jobs face simply because they have low-SES professions.

These results are not encouraging and suggest that even when constituents put forth the same level of effort and articulate the same position, officials assume that high-SES individuals have opinions that are more thoughtful. To the extent that officials are influenced by this factor when taking policy actions, policy will be skewed away from the preferences of low-income voters.

The bias against low-income individuals is also important because previous research shows that political efficacy is an important determinant of political activity. Evidence shows that citizens who have high levels of political efficacy – that is, those who think they have the ability to influence government actions – are much more likely to vote and otherwise participate in political activities that consume time (Verba, Schlozman and Brady 1995, 358). Significantly, low-income and less-educated voters are much less likely to think that their behavior can influence government actions (349).

Based on the finding that low-income individuals have less efficacy, Verba, Schlozman, and Brady (1995) offer the hopeful position that one way to increase the efficacy of underrepresented groups is to persuade them engage in politics as part of a virtuous cycle.

[T]here is reason to believe that participation and engagement are mutually reinforcing: taking part in politics probably enhances political interest, efficacy, and information; reciprocally, these political orientations surely have an impact on participation. (367)

The results presented in this chapter suggest a less hopeful picture. Low-income and less-educated voters may have lower levels of political efficacy because public officials are in fact less responsive to them (see also Bartels 2008; Gilens 2012). Encouraging low-income voters to participate in politics might actually lead them to lead to lower levels of political efficacy. When these voters learn firsthand that it is harder for them to influence government because their opinions are discounted, they may become more disillusioned, not less. This is not to say that efforts should not be put into mobilizing low-income voters or that such efforts cannot yield higher levels of political efficacy; rather, the process is more complicated because public officials are in fact more likely to discount low-income voters' opinions. Increasing low-SES individuals' political efficacy requires both mobilizing them and helping them achieve success in their efforts.

Chapter 4 Appendix

Details of the 2012 American Municipal Officials Survey
Adam Dynes and I jointly conducted the 2012 American Municipal Officials Survey. For the survey we had student research assistants collect the contact

TABLE 4.A1. *Details on Cities in the 2012 American Municipal Officials Survey*

	No E-mails Found	E-mailed but No Response to Survey	Responded to Survey
Number of Municipalities	21,542	2,035	2,989
Population (Census)			
Mean	3,127	17,635	36,304
Median	856	4,523	10,157
Number of Elected Officials			
Mean		5.6	6.6
Median		6	7
Number of Officials with Posted E-mail Addresses			
Mean		75%	92%
Median		100%	100%

information for thousands of city mayors and councilors (or the local equivalents) in cities and towns of all sizes across the United States. The sample of city officials was constructed by first downloading a list of all of the cities in the U.S. Census. The research assistants then searched for the website of each town or city in the census. If they were able to identify the website, they collected the names and e-mail addresses of the mayor and city councilors (or the equivalent).

We created the online survey using Qualtrics and emailed municipal officials a link to the survey. Overall, the survey had a response rate of 20 percent, on a par with recent expert surveys of this nature (e.g., Fisher and Herrick 2013; Harden 2013) and higher than the typical response rate for contemporary telephone surveys of the mass public.

Overall there were three types of municipalities: (1) those that did not have a website with e-mail addresses available,[9] (2) those that did list e-mail addresses but no official accepted the invitation to take the survey, and (3) those in which at least one official took the survey.[10] Table 4.A1 provides the descriptive statistics on the size of these three types of municipalities and shows that the elected officials who took the survey were from systematically larger cities than those who did not. The median municipality for which we could not find any e-mail addresses had a population of only 856 people.

Not only were officials from larger cities more likely to have e-mail addresses listed, but, conditional on having been invited to take the survey, they were also more likely to do so. The median population of cities where no one who

[9] The decision to restrict the sample to city officials with e-mail addresses meant that we also excluded some large cities that provided contact forms in lieu of addresses.

[10] If any of the e-mailed officials responded, the municipality is placed in this category. Thus the response rate "by city" appears to be greater than the response rate by e-mailed official.

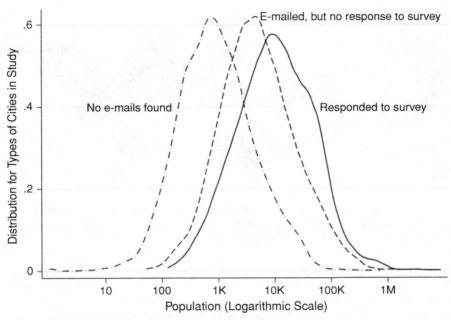

FIGURE 4.A1. Density distribution for cities by response type.

received an invitation took the survey was 4,523. The median population of cities with an official who took the survey was more than double that mark: 10,157. Figure 4.A1 shows the distribution of the population (on a logarithmic scale) for these three types of cities. The pattern clearly shows that our sample is skewed toward larger cities (although it covers cities of all sizes).

Figure 4.A2 displays the geographic dispersion of the responses across the lower forty-eight states for the American Municipal Officials Survey as a whole and shows that there was good geographic coverage across the various regions of the United States.

Details of State Legislator Survey (March 2012)

The survey was conducted in March 2012. The response rate for the survey was about 15 percent (over 1,000 responses total), but I asked the longer survey question presented in this chapter to only a subsample of about 600 legislators. Figure 4.A3 shows the number of respondents who took the survey from each state. There were no responses from Texas and Idaho, where you need to fill out a form that is a screener requiring a within-district address (similar to the United States Congress) to contact each legislator. The darker the color, the larger the number of respondents from that state (the number of responses is listed on the map in the center of each state). The map shows that the survey had fairly good coverage in most states outside of the southwest portion of

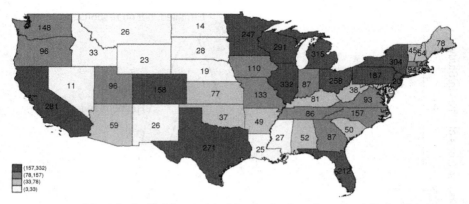

FIGURE 4.A2. Municipal officials participating in the American municipal officials survey. Darker shades indicate that a larger number of respondents were from that state. The actual number of respondents is given in the center of each state.

the country. Further, the legislators come from all levels of legislative professionalism (Squire 2007), with good coverage in highly professional legislatures (e.g., New York, Massachusetts, Pennsylvania, and Illinois), citizen legislatures (e.g., Montana, New Hampshire, Maine, and Utah), and those in between (e.g., Oregon, Missouri, Minnesota, and Connecticut).

Table 4.A2 compares the demographic characteristics of the legislators in the sample (see columns 2 and 3) relative to all state legislators in the United States (column 1). Female legislators and Democratic legislators were more likely to take the survey. In the United States, only 23 percent of the legislators are women, but 32 percent of the legislators who took the survey themselves

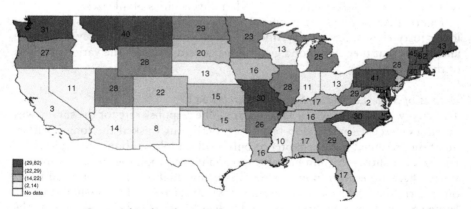

FIGURE 4.A3. Geographic distribution of state legislators participating in the 2012 survey of state legislators. Darker shades indicate that a larger number of respondents were from that state. The actual number of respondents is given in the center of each state.

TABLE 4.A2. *Demographic Makeup of State Legislator Respondents*

	All State Legislators	All Respondents	Self-Identified Legislators
Upper Chamber	26%	25%	22%
Republican	53%	43%	45%
Black	8%	6%	5%
Latino	3%	3%	3%
Female	23%	29%	32%

were women. Similarly, 53 percent of state legislators are Republican but only 45 percent of the legislators who took the survey themselves are Republican. The other characteristics are all within four percentage points of the population average.

In terms of external validity, recent research shows that Internet surveys and traditional mail surveys of state legislators produce similar results (Fisher and Herrick 2013). Further, the distribution of the data in Figure 4.A3 and Table 4.A2 suggest that the sample provides a fairly good picture of state legislators in the United States.

5

Information Costs and Officials' Proactive Effort Levels

Imagine yourself as a mayor. In office you have gained a lot of knowledge about how your community works. But you also have the personal knowledge you brought to office from living in your community and seeing how things work. This personal knowledge helps you perform your duties more efficiently because you have a good understanding of how your city programs run. Consider the local school system. As a longtime community resident, you have likely raised your children in the community and know about some of the programs the local schools offer.

Suppose you receive an e-mail from a Mr. Dan Johnson, who is relocating to your area for work. The Johnson family is comparing different communities to decide where to live, and the father is asking about access to a public library and the programs at the high school. Mr. Johnson could look up this information himself on the school's website, but making people happy is good politics. Can you easily answer his question? Will you take the time to research and answer it? Does your decision to answer depend on which school program Mr. Johnson asks about? Are you more likely to answer if he asks about advanced placement programs rather than free lunch programs?

The Importance of Information

Public officials have limited time and energy and so must carefully choose which issues they will work on. They cannot answer every request for help or tackle every possible issue, even those that seem important to their constituents. They must selectively choose where to focus their energy.

Public officials might decide which issues to focus on based on the information they bring to office. The more information they have, the less time and energy it will take to work on that topic. And the less time it takes to work on an issue, the more likely it is that they will give the issue attention (Hall and

Deardorff 2006). By focusing on areas for which they have an informational advantage, politicians are able to maximize their reelection chances with the fewest resources possible.

Public officials' personal experiences are an important source of the information they bring to office. Individuals from similar demographic groups are likely to have similar experiences because they are likely to face similar challenges or at least know people who do. As a result of this personal experience, officials will give more thought to issues that are important to individuals in their group. Black officials have probably thought more about discrimination in housing. Religiously devout officials may have given more thought to the steps involved in sending children to parochial schools. The knowledge that officials gain from these personal experiences incentivizes them to work on the issues important to constituents who are descriptively like them because it is easier for them to do so.

If legislators' personal backgrounds are an important source of policy-relevant information, then groups that are numerically well represented in office will enjoy better representation because the issues they care about will receive more attention. In other words, one source of inequality in representation may be that policymakers as a whole have less expertise on issues important to groups that are numerically underrepresented and so they work less on those issues. This chapter explores this possibility by testing whether public officials are more likely to take proactive action on issues that are important to constituents who share their descriptive characteristics.

City Mayors, Socioeconomic Status, and Information

Information is an important factor that can affect the thought experiment presented at the beginning of the chapter. Information is important because these mayors are busy. If they need to gather information about their local schools in order to address a query, it means spending less time on other responsibilities – those related to their elected positions, their families, and often their private-sector jobs. If they already have information about the schools, they do not need to divert as much time from other duties; that is, the more information these mayors have about a topic, the less costly it is for them to work on it.

Shang Ha and I implemented the thought experiment with which this chapter began in the spring of 2009. For the experiment, we identified the publicly available e-mail addresses of about a thousand mayors (or the equivalent) who served in small- and medium-sized cities and towns.[1] In early

---

[1] We limited the sample to cities and towns that the U.S. Census considers to be part of a metropolitan area with a population between 1,000 and 150,000 people. For each of these cities, we used the city website to identify its chief executive officer. The mayor or the equivalent (e.g., the village president) was the chief executive officer in over 95 percent of the cities. In a few cities the chief elected official was a city council member or selectman. For each city we e-mailed only one official.

June 2009,[2] each mayor in the sample received the e-mail from the alias Dan Johnson.[3] Each e-mail explained that Mr. Johnson's company was relocating him to the area and the Johnson family was deciding where it wanted to live. Further, each mayor was asked two questions (whether there was a local library and about programs at the high school). The e-mail explained that Mr. Johnson would like a quick response because the family needed to move out of its current housing soon.

Half the mayors in the sample were randomly assigned to receive an e-mail in which Mr. Johnson asked whether the "high school offers a free lunch program" and also indicated that the Johnson family currently rented an apartment. I refer to this as the low-SES treatment.[4] The other half of the mayors received an e-mail that asked whether the "high school offers advanced placement programs" and indicated that the Johnson family currently owned a home. I refer to this as the high-SES treatment.

Where Do Mayors Get Information?

A key difference between the low-SES and high-SES treatments is that they ask about different programs. The immediate goal is to test whether there is evidence that the information mayors brought to office affects their ability to answer the two questions about the local high school. The larger goal is to discover whether relevant preexisting differences in information affect elected officials' behavior in office.

There are reasons to think that personal information might not matter. Elected officials might actively engage in learning about issues that are relevant to constituents who are not like them – but do they? In this case, there is a testable null hypothesis. If there are no differences among elected officials in terms of the information they have about an issue, there should be no differences in how costly it is for them to answer a question about the issue; that is, the information costs should be homogeneous. This implies that elected officials should all be equally responsive to the questions about the different school programs. If, however, personal information does matter, then the elected officials who have more information on the topic because of their own backgrounds should be more responsive.

---

[2] The main reason we sent the e-mails in June is that it fit the narrative described in the message. The e-mail suggests that Mr. Johnson has school-age children and would be looking for housing in the area immediately. This fits because the Johnson family would be waiting for the school year to end before moving and because June is part of the primary housing market season for homebuyers with children.

[3] Even though all the e-mails were sent from the same alias, we were not worried that this would lead to detection of the experiment because it is unlikely that mayors from neighboring jurisdictions talk to each other about the e-mails they receive. Even if they do discuss their e-mails, the message itself suggests that Mr. Johnson will be contacting officials in a number of cities to find the one that best meets his family's needs.

[4] To ensure that we had balance with the size and wealth of the town, we block randomized on the median household income and population of the town.

In our experiment, where might the mayors' information about school programs come from? The responses we received from the mayors in the experiment suggested at least two major sources.

First, several mayors indicated that they had information about the school system because they worked in the schools. For example:

My wife and I both work at [redacted] High School (25 years) and we do offer Advanced Placement Classes.

I should let you know that I am not only the mayor, but also was the chair of the task force that led the library project through the process, and am a teacher at [name of high school redacted], so I have insights into both of the questions you asked.

An even larger number of public officials cited their experiences with their own children as the source of their information about the local high school. Numerous mayors who were asked whether the local high school offered advanced placement courses referred to the experiences of their children. Here is a small sample of those responses.

Hi Dan
[City name redacted] has a library and . . . does offer some AP courses but I have only the specific knowledge of my daughter taking them.

[M]y daughter just graduated from [redacted] High School. She enjoyed a number of their AP courses and we found that the school was fantastic.

My son will be a senior there [at the local high school] and . . . has taken Honors and AP classes.

Regarding your second question, yes the [redacted] School District does offer AP classes, both of my sons have taken advantage of these classes.

Public officials with such personal information do not have to invest time in research and can directly answer the questions. They are also more confident in their answers. This can be seen in one of the responses we received from a mayor without this type of firsthand experience.

I do believe the local high schools have AP (my son is only 5 right now, so I am sorry I do not know better first hand).

At least some of the mayors clearly used their personal experiences to answer questions. How does this information explain why mayors respond to one question more often than the other?

In our experiment, the information that comes from on-the-job experience is not likely to make a difference for our questions. Mayors who work as teachers are likely to be equally informed about the questions posed in both the low-SES and high-SES treatments. Their job experience should not make them more likely to respond to one question than the other.

In contrast, the information that mayors gained from the experiences of their own children and their friends' children is likely to influence their relative ability to answer the questions. We expected the mayors in high-SES communities to be less likely to know about free lunch programs. Their own children, as well as their friends' children, are simply less likely to have participated in such programs. Mayors from low-SES communities, by contrast, should be more likely to personally know high school students who have used the resources of this type of program. Our expectation was that a similar pattern might also explain individuals' knowledge about advanced placement programs at the high school. Mayors from high-SES communities might be more likely to personally know high school students – possibly their own children – who took advanced placement courses.

If information matters, then increases in the median household income of the city should lead to an increase in the relative number of mayors who answer the question regarding the advanced placement program compared with the number of mayors who answer the question regarding the free lunch program. Before testing this prediction, it is worth considering a number of questions that naturally arise about this experiment.

Why Education? Why City Mayors?

We focus on education because most individuals have personal experience on which to draw. Most mayors have either raised their own children or have friends who raised children in the local school system.

Education is also one of the largest expenditures in most city budgets. About a third of all local government spending in the United States goes to elementary and secondary education (Census of Governments 2007). Because education is a local issue, studying city officials makes sense for this topic.

Another reason to study city mayors is that they have responsibility for the entire city, whereas state legislators develop expertise in their committees' jurisdictions.[5] Specialization is not a problem in and of itself. But if legislators are more likely to serve on committees that concern policy areas most relevant to their constituents (Fenno 1973; Weingast and Marshall 1988; Adler and Lapinski 1997) and those constituents happen to elect descriptive representatives, then the relationship between descriptive representation and legislators' information could be spurious. The correlation could simply reflect the fact that legislators choose committees that help them develop expertise on a topic their constituents care about.

There are potential downsides to looking at mayors instead of legislators. As David Mayhew writes, "[E]lected legislators are basically position takers.

---

[5] In the constituency service field experiment I ran on state legislators for this chapter, one legislator explained that he or she was unable to answer a question about taxes because "my work in the legislature mostly focused on education issues and I have not served on a tax committee." This is anecdotal evidence that the information that legislators gain from their committee assignments may affect their responsiveness.

Elected executives are basically managers" (2008, 203). Because mayors have more managerial responsibility than state legislators do, they may be better prepared to deal with questions from constituents. As a result, we may underestimate the degree to which information affects representation.

What about Possible Discrimination against Low-Income Constituents?

One obstacle to drawing conclusions from this study is that results might be driven by other information that the mayors inferred from the text of the e-mail. Mayors might respond differently to questions about the two different school programs because the question itself reveals something about the writer, and they might use that information to infer the writer's SES. Mayors who are asked whether the school offers a free lunch program are more likely to assume that Dan Johnson is of a lower SES than mayors who are asked about the existence of an advanced placement program. The e-mail reinforces this by signaling something about the Johnson family's current housing arrangement.

Because the treatments signal different things about the sender's likely SES, the mayors' responses could be affected by their attitudes toward low- and high-SES individuals. The next chapter presents evidence that state legislators exhibit a personal, in-group bias in favor of constituents of their own race/ethnicity. It is possible that mayors exhibit the same type of discrimination by SES. Previous studies have suggested that federal officials, who tend to be of higher SES themselves, favor high-SES individuals in the speeches they make (Druckman and Jacobs 2011), the votes they take (Bartels 2008; cf. Erikson and Bhatti 2011), and the policies they favor (Gilens 2005; Rigby and Wright 2011; cf. Wlezien and Soroka 2011). Wealthy individuals are more likely to know about issues, have clear preferences, participate in politics, and donate money to candidates (APSA Task Force 2004). Because candidates need money and voters who show up on Election Day in order to win, elections should only exacerbate any bias toward high-SES individuals. Further, mayors have a powerful structural incentive to have wealthy rather than poor families move into their communities because it deepens the tax base and leads to fewer expenses (Gramlich and Laren 1984; Peterson and Rom 1989, 1990). These concerns would have been particularly salient in 2009 and 2010, when this study was conducted, because many localities were dealing with budget shortfalls at the time.

If mayors exhibit a personal, in-group bias for people closer to their own socioeconomic group, we would expect that increases in the median household income of the city will lead to an increase in the relative number of mayors who answer the question regarding the advanced placement program compared to the number of mayors who answer the question regarding the free lunch program. This is the same result we would expect if mayors use information from their own experiences to answer the question. In sum, the treatment is possibly confounding two ways in which citizens' SES might influence how

---

BOX 5.1. **E-mail Sent to Mayors in 2009**

From: Dan Johnson

To: [official's e-mail address]

Subject: A Question about [official's city]

Dear [official's position] [official's last name],

My name is Dan Johnson and my company is relocating me and my family to [official's state] and we are trying to decide where to live. I had two quick questions about [official's city] that I thought you might know the answer to: First, does [official's city] have its own public library? Second, do you know if the high school offers [*advanced placement programs / a free lunch program*]?

   If you could reply soon, it would be really helpful as [*we close on our house / our rental contract ends*] at the end of the month and we are trying to make a decision soon.

Thank you very much.
Dan

Notes: Items in bold were manipulated across e-mails. Items in italics were assigned randomly based on the treatment group. The low-SES treatment e-mail included the "a free lunch program" and "our rental contract ends" language while the high-SES treatment e-mail included the "advanced placement programs" and "we close on our house" language.

---

mayors respond: mayors' in-group bias in favor of citizens closer to their own SES, and mayors having knowledge about issues that are important to citizens from a similar socioeconomic background.

Separating the Effect of Information from the Effect of In-Group Bias
We could not adjudicate between the information and in-group bias stories by manipulating the question because the question itself signals something about the sender's SES. However, we took two steps to increase our confidence that any result we found would be driven by differences in the information mayors have, and not mayors' in-group, personal bias.

   First, we asked the library question in the same way across treatments (see Box 5.1). If in-group bias explains the differences in the way people respond to the schools question, we should see differences in overall responsiveness and how well mayors answer the question about the community library. However, if the bias exists because mayors have less knowledge about low-SES issues, we should only see differences in how responsive they were to the question about the local high school.

   Second, we ran a follow-up experiment in the spring of 2010 in which we held the question constant and used other information to signal the SES of the individual sending the e-mail (see Box 5.2). The 2010 study serves as a

---

BOX 5.2. **E-mail Sent to Mayors in 2010**

From: Andy Hansen

To: [**official's e-mail address**]

Subject: A Question about [**official's city**]

Dear [**official's position**] [**official's last name**],

I recently accepted a [*janitorial / managerial*] position at a company in your area and am considering trying to [*rent an apartment / buy a home*] in your town. As we compare different locations, I am trying to learn about whether you have a car tax or any other fees in [**official's city**].

Thanks,
Andy Hansen

Notes: Items in bold were manipulated across e-mails. Items in italics were assigned randomly based on the treatment group. The low-SES treatment e-mail included the "janitorial" and "rent an apartment" language while the high-SES treatment e-mail included the "managerial" and "buy a home" language.

---

placebo test. If information explains the results of the 2009 (see Box 5.1) study, we should find that low- and high-SES individuals are treated the same in the 2010 study.

In the follow-up study we also tried to correct for other concerns about the 2009 study. We worried that the socioeconomic signals in the 2009 study were not strong enough. Because the e-mail indicated that the father's employer was relocating the Johnson family, the city official may have assumed that this individual was in the middle class. Dan Johnson also indicated what the family's housing situation was, not what he expected it to become. Also, because the e-mail indicated that Johnson had children, city officials may have chosen not to engage in discrimination simply because children were involved.

Our second experiment followed a protocol similar to that used in the first experiment. We used the same sample of cities and again e-mailed the city's chief executive, typically the mayor. The text of the e-mail appears in Box 5.2. All e-mails were sent using the alias Andy Hansen and asked whether the city had a car tax or any other fees. All the elected officials were asked the same question because we wanted to test whether individuals' SES affected the way legislators treated them without confounding any effects that might result from asking different types of questions. We asked about a car tax because most individuals, regardless of their income, own cars. Also, the question is general enough to be plausibly important to nearly everyone and addresses an issue that is often dealt with at the municipal level.

In the second experiment we signaled the sender's SES by randomizing information about his job and desired housing situation in the text of the e-mail.

TABLE 5.1. *Socioeconomic Bias among Mayors in 2009 and 2010*

(A) June 2009 Experiment

			Answered Question	
	Responded	Timely Response	Library	School
Low-SES Treatment	77.1%	74.5%	74.8%	52.9%
High-SES Treatment	75.5%	72.1%	74.2%	62.3%
Difference	1.6	2.4	0.6	−9.6**
(Std. Error)	(2.6)	(2.7)	(2.7)	(3.0)
Obs.	1,060	1,060	1,060	1,060

(B) April 2010 Experiment

	Responded	Timely Response	Answered Question
Low-SES Treatment	61.1%	57.6%	59.0%
High-SES Treatment	62.6%	59.8%	59.8%
Difference	−1.5	−2.2	−0.8
(Std. Error)	(2.9)	(3.0)	(3.0)
Observations	1,092	1,092	1,092

Notes: **Sig at the 0.01 level (one-tailed); *Sig at the 0.05 level (one-tailed). Standard errors of the estimated differences are given in parentheses. The sample for both studies is the chief elected executive (typically the mayor) in cities and towns located in metropolitan areas with populations between 1,000 and 150,000 people. Each elected official received a short e-mail (see Box 5.1 for the June 2009 experiment and Box 5.2 for the April 2010 experiment) in which we randomized whether the e-mail signaled that the putative constituent was low-SES or high-SES.

The city officials assigned to the low-SES treatment received an e-mail indicating that the sender was a janitor who would be renting an apartment. The high-SES individual indicated that he was a manager looking to buy a home. These e-mails were sent in the first week of April 2010.

The Results for the Two SES Studies on Mayors

For both the 2009 and 2010 experiments, I present three outcomes: *responded* measures whether the official provided a response at all, *timely response* measures whether the official responded within two weeks, and *answered question* measures whether the official provided a response that answered the question. Because the e-mails sent in the 2009 study asked two questions (see Box 5.1), I separately analyze whether the officials answered these questions.

Table 5.1 shows the average differences between the low- and high-SES treatments in both experiments. Each cell gives the percentage of city officials in the treatment condition that provided a response meeting the criteria for the dependent variable. I also list the percentage point difference between the responses to the low- and high-SES treatments, with the associated standard error given in parentheses.

The results show that the vast majority of mayors responded. In the June 2009 study, 77.1 percent of mayors who received the low-SES e-mail responded, and 75.5 percent of the mayors who received the high-SES e-mail responded. The 1.6 percentage point difference is not statistically significant. Similar results hold for the 2010 study. Mayors responded to both the low- and high-SES e-mails just over 60 percent of the time.

In both experiments, the mayors respond to the low- and high-SES individuals at equal rates. Mayors are also equally likely to provide timely responses to both low- and high-SES individuals. Finally, mayors are equally likely to answer the questions that are held constant across the e-mails: the library question in the 2009 study and the tax question in the 2010 study. When holding the question constant, the city officials were equally responsive to both the low- and the high-SES individuals.

Does this mean that mayors do not exhibit a socioeconomic-based personal bias? Not necessarily. It may be that mayors from poorer cities are more responsive to low-SES individuals and mayors from wealthier cities are more responsive to high-SES individuals but on average there are no differences.

Figure 5.1 shows that the level of socioeconomic bias did not vary with the median household income of the mayor's city for the outcomes *responded* and *timely response*. For each panel in the figure I used locally weighted regression (lowess) to estimate the predicted probabilities, with the dashed (solid) line representing the lowess line for the low-SES (high-SES) treatment group. The histograms show the distribution of mayors included in the study by the median household income of their cities. The top half of Figure 5.1 presents the results for the 2009 study showing that low-SES individuals are treated slightly worse in cities with median household incomes above ninety thousand dollars. However, this difference is not statistically significant. Further, in the 2010 results – in the bottom half of the figure – this pattern reverses itself. The mayors from the wealthiest cities were, if anything, more responsive to e-mails from low-SES individuals. Again, however, this difference is not statistically significant. Taken together, these results (combined with those in Table 5.1) show no evidence of an in-group, personal bias among city mayors.

The results for whether the mayors answered the questions raised in the e-mails, however, suggest that socioeconomic descriptive representation affects how easy it is to answer constituents' questions. The results in Table 5.1 show that in the 2010 study, where the question about taxes was held constant across the socioeconomic treatments, the mayors were equally likely to answer the question in both socioeconomic treatments. The same is true for the library question in the 2009 study. In contrast, mayors who received the low-SES question about the availability of a free lunch program were nearly ten percentage points less likely – a statistically significant difference – to answer that question than mayors who were asked about the availability of advanced placement courses. This difference is consistent with the possibility

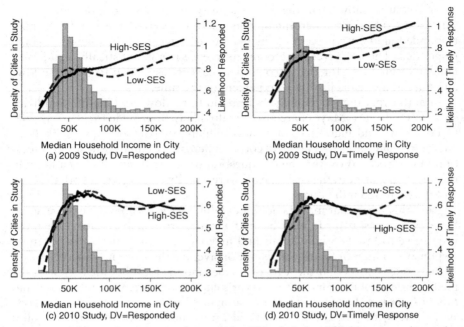

FIGURE 5.1. Mayors' treatment of e-mails by SES of sender. The histogram shows the distribution of the median household income across the cities in the sample. The lines, which give the likelihood that the city official answered the question he or she was asked, are estimated using lowess regressions. The dashed (solid) line gives the lowess line for the low-SES (high-SES) treatment.

that mayors have more knowledge about high-SES issues due to personal experience.

Alternatively, mayors may have been more responsive to the high-SES question because it was simply an easier question to answer. Of course, this possibility is interrelated with the mayor's knowledge drawn from firsthand experience. The high-SES school question may have been easier to answer *because* mayors, who are more likely to be high-SES individuals themselves, are more likely to have had firsthand experience with advanced placement courses than with free lunch programs. This is exactly how information may explain the benefits that come to constituents through descriptive representation.

If descriptive representation explains why the high-SES question is answered more frequently, then we should observe a heterogeneous treatment effect with respect to the wealth of the city for how well the low- and high-SES school questions are answered. The library question in the 2009 study and the tax question in the 2010 study provide placebo tests for this argument; there should be no interactive effect between the wealth of the city and whether these questions are answered.

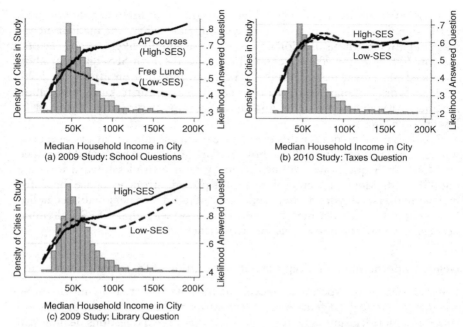

FIGURE 5.2. Responsiveness by SES treatment and wealth of the city. The histogram shows the distribution of the median household income across the cities in the sample. The lines, which give the likelihood that the city official answered the question he or she was asked, are estimated using lowess regressions. The dashed (solid) line gives the lowess line for the low-SES (high-SES) treatment.

Figure 5.2 shows how the outcome *question answered* varied with the median household income of the city the mayor represented for each of the three questions. For each panel in the figure I use locally weighted regression (lowess) to estimate the predicted probabilities, with the dashed (solid) line representing the lowess line for the low-SES (high-SES) treatment group. The histograms show the distribution of mayors included in the study by the median household income of their cities. Panels (b) and (c) of Figure 5.2 show our placebo tests using the question for the 2010 tax question and 2009 library question, respectively. In both cases the wealth of the city did not moderate the difference in how likely the mayors were to answer the low-SES versus high-SES questions.

The results in panel (a) in Figure 5.2, however, show that mayors from wealthier cities had a much harder time answering the question about free lunch. In cities where the median household income exceeded fifty thousand dollars, there is a sharp divergence in how well the two questions were answered. The wealthier the city the more likely the mayor was to answer the question about advanced placement courses and the less likely the mayor was to answer the question about free lunch programs (a difference that is statistically significant). By contrast, the mayors of cities where the median income was roughly fifty thousand dollars or less were equally likely to answer both the low-SES question about school lunch and the high-SES question about advanced placement classes. Mayors' personal information affects the issues they can work on: mayors in wealthier situations appear to know more about advanced placement programs and much less about programs designed for low-income citizens.

Recall that we do not see this divergence on the library or car tax questions, which suggests that differences in how mayors respond to advanced placement and free lunch questions are not driven by their attitudes toward low- and high-SES individuals. Together these results provide strong evidence that information matters. Mayors do not seem to exhibit a direct personal bias against low-income individuals, but they do better represent higher-SES individuals because of their own knowledge and experience.

Gender, Information, and Representation: A Study of State Legislators

I also conducted an experiment to evaluate the possibility that an informational advantage would lead female state legislators to be relatively more responsive – and male legislators relatively less responsive – to questions dealing with women's issues than to other questions. I conducted this experiment to see whether the results from the constituency service field experiments on mayors could be applied to other public officials and other questions.

Why Run a Constituency Service Field Experiment?

Previous studies found evidence consistent with the possibility that female legislators substantively better represent female constituents due to information. Researchers have found that women participate more in floor debates on women's issues (Tamerius 1995) and committees with more women are more likely to produce legislation that incorporates women's interests (Berkman and O'Connor 1993; Dodson 1998; Norton 1999; Swers 2002). Given these findings, what is the advantage of running a constituency service field experiment?

The previous observational studies have not controlled for legislators' opportunities to deal with women's issues. Female legislators may advocate women's interests because they have more knowledge or information about these issues. Alternatively, they may simply have more opportunities to become involved. Committee assignments structure the opportunities that legislators have to focus on issues (Fenno 1973), and female legislators in both the United States (Diamond 1977; Thomas and Welch 1991; Thomas 1994; Darcy 1996) and elsewhere (Considine and Deutchman 1994; Heath, Schwindt-Bayer, and Taylor-Robinson 2005) are more likely to serve on committees focused on women's issues.

The constituency service field experiment ensures that the differences in legislators' opportunities are not driving the results because I randomized the subject of each letter. This research design also avoids the problems that can arise from using surveys, such as social desirability bias.

Research Design for the 2010 Study on Information and Gender

Omitted variable bias is also a concern because men and women, on average, represent different districts (Palmer and Simon 2006). These differences might affect legislators' information and thus lead to differences in the way they respond to e-mail requests. I mitigate this concern by using the logic of a regression discontinuity design to construct the sampling frame (see Butler and Butler 2006; Imbens and Lemieux 2008; Lee 2008). In this study I compare men and women legislators who won competitive elections against a candidate of the opposite gender. The reason for comparing a close election is that these outcomes are often determined by idiosyncratic factors. Thus the results can be treated as if the outcome were randomly determined. It also means that factors not associated with the gender of the legislator, such as constituent preferences, should be, on average, quite similar for the two groups of legislators.

I used information from the Center for American Women and Politics at Rutgers University to identify all the legislators serving in the spring of 2010 who competed against a candidate of the other gender in the most recent general election (Center for American Women and Politics 2011). For these races I measured the percentage of the two-candidate vote share the female candidate received,[6] collecting a sample that included 197 legislators who won their previous elections with 52.5 percent or less of the vote.

I conducted a constituency service field experiment on the legislators I identified by sending each of them a short e-mail that began with a formal salutation ("Dear [representative's title and last name]"), asked a simple constituency service question, and finished with a formal ending signed with the randomly chosen alias. In total I created twenty aliases with corresponding e-mail accounts.[7] For each e-mail I randomized the question that was asked. As with the aliases, there were a total of twenty questions. Table 5.2 contains a list of the questions.

---

[6] In this case, the female candidate's two-candidate vote share is that for the top vote-getting female divided by the total received by her and the top vote-getting male.

[7] I randomized the alias used when contacting each legislator. I chose to use only white-sounding names because whites represent the largest group of voters. I chose a total of ten male and ten female aliases. These names were generated using lists of common first and last names among self-identified whites (Fryer and Levitt 2004; Word et al. n.d.).

The male aliases used in this study were Andrew Kelly, Dennis Powell, Eric Gray, Gregory Wood, Jerry Jenkins, Joshua Ross, Patrick Butler, Ray Price, Stephen Watson, and Walter Patterson.

The female aliases were Amy Bennett, Angela James, Anna Barnes, Brenda Sanders, Cynthia Peterson, Kathleen Long, Melissa Brooks, Pam Hughes, Rebecca Coleman, and Virginia Perry.

TABLE 5.2. *Questions Used in the Gender Study*

	Question	Women's Issue?	Low SES?
1	Is there any way to find out how the well different schools perform on required state tests? I want to check the performance of schools across districts.	Yes	No
2	I recently moved within the state and am wondering about what I need to do in order to transfer my voter registration to my new residence.	No	No
3	My child will start school next year and I'm trying to learn what immunizations they need. Do you know that information or where I might find it?	Yes	No
4	I realize that the election is still a ways off, but I'm still wondering about whether there is a deadline to register to vote?	No	No
5	I have a child who will be starting school soon and I'm wondering what I need to do to enroll them.	Yes	No
6	What steps do I need to take if I want to vote absentee in the next election?	No	No
7	We are expecting a baby several months away and I was trying to figure out maternity leave. What are the state laws regarding the length of maternity leave?	Yes	No
8	We just moved into the area and I am trying to figure out how to find my polling place. Is there a site that lists the location of polling places?	No	No
9	I was wondering whether the state has any programs to help with childcare after my kids are out of school.	Yes	No
10	Does the state list anywhere the jobs in state government? I'm interested in finding out what is available.	No	No
11	We are expecting our first child soon and one of my friends told me I should apply for WIC. Do you know how I do that?	Yes	Yes
12	Do you know whether people who are working are also eligible for food stamps?	Maybe	Yes
13	What are the requirements to get health coverage from the state for children under 16? I want to see whether my friend's family qualifies.	Yes	Yes
14	Can someone receive both social security income and unemployment? I am trying to help a friend out.	Maybe	Yes
15	Do you know whether the state-provided health insurance covers pregnancy expenses even if our family enrolled after the pregnancy?	Yes	Yes
16	It looks like I may soon lose my job as a janitor and I'm wondering how I apply for unemployment.	Maybe	Yes
17	We recently had a child and are going to be breastfeeding. What are the laws about getting breaks for breastfeeding at work? Do women get breaks to do so?	Yes	No
18	I just sold my home and am wondering how I report the sale of a home on my taxes. Do I have to do anything at this point about that?	No	No
19	A friend was telling me that in some states health insurance companies are required to cover fertility treatments. Is that true here?	Yes	No
20	I'm worried that I won't be able to finish my taxes before the deadline. Do you know whether I can apply for an extension (and how I should do that)?	No	No

Why Use These Twenty Questions in the Experiment?

I used a total of twenty questions and twenty aliases because I limited the number of legislators in the sample from each legislative chamber to twenty. Because I block randomized on each state and legislative chamber, I only used each alias once per chamber, and no legislators in the same chamber were asked the same question.

Of the twenty different questions used in the experiment, ten were intended to deal with women's issues and ten dealt with other topics. In writing the questions, I tried to follow the convention in the literature of classifying health, welfare, and education as women's issues (Saint-Germain 1989; Swers 1998, 2002). The other questions in the experiment focused on issues related to voting, employment, and taxes.

In writing the questions dealing with women's issues and other topics, I tried to make them comparable along other dimensions. Because the welfare questions all signaled that the person asking the question had a low SES, I tried to create questions that dealt with employment and also signaled that the individual had a low SES. Questions 12, 14, and 16 (see Table 5.2) were meant to deal primarily with employment, but they could also be classified as welfare issues. As a result, it is not clear whether these questions should be classified as dealing with women's issues or not. For this reason, I present the results when excluding these questions from the analysis.[8] The results are substantively similar when these questions are used in the analysis.

What about In-Group, Personal Bias?

In the case of the education study described earlier, it was difficult to separate the content of the question from any potential socioeconomic bias. The question itself sends a signal about the writer's potential SES.

By contrast, we can easily signal the putative gender of the writer separately from the question asked. The experimentally manipulated name signals the constituent's gender. Consequently, it is easy to test the information mechanism separately from considerations about the writer's gender.

Results for the Gender Experiment

Table 5.3 presents the results for how the issue affected legislators' responsiveness to constituents' questions. The difference between the way women's issues and other issues are treated is given in percentage point terms at the bottom of each section, with the standard errors given in parentheses. These values are calculated so that positive values indicate a differential treatment in favor of women's issues and negative values a differential treatment in favor of other issues. I present the results without the three questions that did not fit neatly

---

[8] It is worth noting that I randomized which question was used in each e-mail; that is, the questions were randomized within the issue treatment.

TABLE 5.3. *Responsiveness by Request Type (Women's Issue vs. Other Issue)*

	Female Legislators			Male Legislators		
	Respond	Timely Response	Answered Question	Respond	Timely Response	Answered Question
Women's Issue	61.1%	57.4%	42.6%	47.7%	41.0%	22.7%
Other Issue	65.7%	57.1%	54.3%	75.8%	75.8%	51.5%
Difference	−4.6	0.3	−11.7	−28.0**	−34.8**	−28.8**
(Std. Error)	(10.6)	(10.9)	(10.9)	(11.0)	(10.9)	(10.6)
Observations	89	89	89	77	77	77

Notes: ** Sig at the 0.01 level (one-tailed), *Sig at the 0.05 level (one-tailed). The percentages in the table are the percentage of the legislators whose responses met the requirements for the measured outcome. All the legislators in the sample faced a candidate of the opposite gender in their most recent general election and won with 52.5 percent or less of the two-candidate vote total.

into either category (i.e., questions 12, 14, and 16 in Table 5.2), though the results are substantively similar when these questions are included. Finally, I show the results broken down by gender in order to test whether men are less responsive to the women's issues (as opposed to other issues).

The results in Table 5.3 show that female legislators were equally responsive to questions on both issues. For the questions dealing with women's issues the women's response rate was 61 percent, and for questions on other topics the response rate was just under 66 percent. Surprisingly this result actually goes in the unexpected direction: women in the study were less responsive to the women's issues questions (though the difference is statistically insignificant). This does not mean that women necessarily prioritize these other issues. It may be that the specific questions dealing with women's issues were simply harder questions for everyone. Consistent with this possibility, we see that the male legislators were also less responsive to the questions dealing with women's issues.

Significantly, Table 5.3 shows that male legislators showed a much stronger disinclination than female legislators to respond to questions about women's issues. While the men responded to only 48 percent of the questions dealing with women's issues, they responded to about 76 percent of the other questions. This large thirty percentage point difference is statistically significant. Male legislators were also nearly thirty percentage points less likely to send responses that arrived in a timely manner or to answer the question if it dealt with a women's issue.[9]

Although we must be careful in interpreting the findings, it is clear that, at least in relative terms, women prioritize women's issues more than men do.

[9] Although they are not shown here, the results also hold when controlling for the legislator's partisanship. That roughly two-thirds of the female legislators in the sample are Democrats does not drive the observed findings.

We can only make claims about legislators' relative prioritization because our questions dealing with women's issues may simply have been harder questions that suppressed the level of responsiveness for everyone. It may be that men put less effort into women's issues and women put equal effort into all issues, or it may be that men put equal effort into all issues and women prioritize women's issues. Either way, the results clearly show that female legislators, compared with their male counterparts, are relatively more responsive to questions about women's issues than to other questions.

What the State Legislators Wrote
Combined with the results from the two mayoral studies, the findings are evidence that descriptive representation matters, at least in part, because of the knowledge that representatives bring to office. The text of the responses that public officials sent is consistent with this view. Many officials referred to information they had gathered as a result of firsthand experience in either their professional or personal lives. Compare, for example, the responses from state legislators who were asked about whether the putative constituents needed to do anything about taxes on the homes they had just sold (see question 18 in Table 5.2).

I'm not a tax attorney, but I recall when I sold my home, that as long as I purchased another home within two years, I didn't have to pay capitol gains on the equity. I also know, that if you did a short sale you can claim the loss of equity.

I would advise you to call the IRS question hot-line and ask the question or contact an tax attorney and ask the question.

Our office has recd your email and recommend you contact a tax advisor. We are not aware of the particulars of your personal finances nor do we feel knowledgeable enough to render tax advise.

Thank you for your e-mail. Unfortunately I am not a CPA and I do not want give the wrong tax advice. I appreciate your request and would suggest contacting a CPA or going to the IRS website at www.IRS.gov They have a FAQ section which includes information on selling your home. I believe the site also has a phone number to call for tax advice. I hope this information is helpful and I am sorry I could not give you any direct tax advice.

I really can't answer that. I have never sold a home. I would suggest you go to a tax preparer and ask the question.

All the legislators prudently advised the constituent to get help from the IRS or a professional. However, the first legislator also drew on his own experience to provide information on the question. As the following snippets from other e-mails show, similar responses to other questions came from numerous legislators.
[In response to a question about voting absentee:]

I have never voted by absentee ballot, but I believe that I would contact the Supervisor of the checklist . . .

[On the issue of seeking a tax filing extension:]

I am not an accountant. But, I have applied for and received extension from IRS...

[About breast-feeding at work:]

I do not know of any laws that deny women from breastfeeding during a break but there are laws against breast feeding in public.

As a former Human resource Manager, I have never came across this issue but there must be something in the company policy on breastfeeding.

This issue comes up from time to time and I learned a whole lot more about it when my wife and I had our first child...

[Tax reporting for renting out a house:]

I am not a tax expert, but I did rent out a portion of my house a number of years ago. The most important thing is to...

[About the do-not-call list (from Chapter 3):]

All of my phone numbers are on the do not call list and I repeatedly get calls from surveys and solicitors. Apparently, Congress has a loop hole that once the caller elect to have their number identified, they can continue to call your number even if it is registered with the do not call list.

Sometimes I don't know why Congress pass laws in the name of making things better, there always seem to be loop holes for every law they pass.

What I do to avoid these calls is...

Public officials are not blank slates when they come to office. They use knowledge from their own experiences – both professional and personal – to aid constituents seeking help.

Discussion

Some constituents are at a disadvantage because their representatives do not have the information that incentivizes them to work on issues they care about. Legislators' proactive actions are important because these actions shape political outcomes and affect representation (Hall 1996; Burden 2007). Before a bill can be voted on, the issue it deals with must be researched, the bill must be drafted, politicians must debate the issue, and so on. If some issues are never discussed and considered, the groups that care about those issues will be underrepresented. On a more individual level, the constituents who need help in these areas will also be at a disadvantage because their elected officials will lack the incentive to help them – doing so requires too much effort!

In contrast, when politicians have firsthand experience with an issue, they work more on that issue because it is less costly for them to do so. Shang Ha and I showed that city mayors, who tend to come from wealthier backgrounds, are more likely to answer a high-SES than a low-SES question. Further, a mayor's likelihood of responding was moderated by the wealth of the city: the wealthier the city, the more likely the mayor was to answer our high-SES question and the less likely to answer our low-SES question.

I also conducted an experiment looking at responsiveness by gender and found that female legislators, relative to their male colleagues, put relatively more effort into women's issues. This is consistent with previous research suggesting that women legislators put more effort into issues that are considered women's issues than their male counterparts do (Dodson and Carroll 1991; Dolan and Ford 1995; Gertzog 1995; Foerstel and Foerstel 1996).

Because politicians appear to work more on issues with which they have personal experience (see Bratton and Haynie 1999; Swers 2002; review in Swers and Rouse 2011), groups that are numerically underrepresented will also be disadvantaged in terms of their representation. With fewer women, minorities, and low-income representatives in office, issues of importance to these groups will receive less attention because fewer legislators will proactively research these issues, propose bills on these topics, provide good information during deliberations on these issues, help constituents who need help with them, and so on. The lack of individuals with personal expertise to proactively advocate for the issues that low-income and minority voters care about contributes to (or at least compounds) the underrepresentation of these groups.

How Many Representatives Are Needed?
Increasing the numerical representation of some groups means decreasing the representation of other groups. How, then, can we decide whether the benefits of increasing the representation of one group outweighs the costs to other groups? Rosabeth Moss Kanter (1977), and subsequent researchers, argued that a critical mass is needed to activate the benefits of descriptive representation (Kanter suggested 15 percent as a critical threshold). Contradictory findings since then have raised questions about the usefulness of the notion of a critical mass (Bratton 2005; Grey 2006; Beckwith 2007; see also review in Swers and Rouse 2011).

My experiments do not provide any new insights into questions about critical thresholds. Still, by the proportionality standard, women, minorities, and low-SES individuals are underrepresented. The results in this chapter suggest that decreasing the bias in numerical representation for these groups will likely improve their substantive representation because legislators will collectively put more effort into issues important to these citizens.

Information as a Collective Benefit
The informational benefits that come with the increased representation of politically disadvantaged groups can be a collective benefit. In several cases,

the politicians I studied relied on each other to serve their constituents. For example, when we asked the mayor's office in one city whether the local high school offered advanced placement courses, the office redirected the e-mail to a city council member who had personal experience with AP courses at the high school. As the city council member wrote:

I'm a member of City Council with a student who just graduated High School last week, so I've been asked to answer your question. While I'm not a school district employee, and cannot officially answer your question, my quick response to your advance placement question would be to say yes. [There follows a full paragraph on the joint college–high school program available at the school.]

State legislators also relied on the expertise of other members. One forwarded an e-mail to another representative with this preface: "This is from another member of the House that is an attorney that specializes in this area." Another wrote that he had forwarded the question "to another representative who is more versed in insurance."

The results show that the information that legislators bring to office because of their personal experience benefits not only their constituents but also the constituents in other districts because legislators rely on each other for information. As the informational advantage is also likely to affect how legislators develop policy, it also explains one of the benefits of descriptive representation for racial minorities – or any minority group, for that matter. Legislators who represent a small minority are unlikely to either affect the agenda or prove pivotal on a large number of votes (Grose 2011); however, even a small number of minority legislators can provide benefits to all constituents like them because they focus more on issues important to those constituents.

No Personal Bias Related to Socioeconomic Status

Although we found evidence of an informational advantage among city mayors, there is no evidence that mayors exhibit a direct bias against individuals based on their SES. The lack of such discrimination is surprising for several reasons. First, several previous studies have suggested that public officials exhibit a bias toward the wealthy (Bartels 2008; Gilens 2005, 2009, 2012; cf. Wlezien and Soroka 2011). Second, wealthy individuals are more likely to have the financial and political resources that candidates need to win reelection (APSA Task Force 2004). Third, researchers have argued that governments compete with each other to provide the fewest social services so as to discourage low-income individuals from moving into their jurisdictions (Gramlich and Laren 1984; Peterson and Rom 1989, 1990). These factors should have only compounded any personal bias that might exist. In other words, if government officials have a personal bias against low-SES individuals, it should have been easiest to observe among city officials. Yet we find no evidence of a direct bias against low-income citizens.

When taken with the results in Chapter 4, we see that the bias against low-income citizens occurs at the input stage, not the output stage. Public officials discount the opinions of low-SES individuals, but they do not exhibit a direct bias against them at the output stage. In the next chapter I present experiments that test whether there is evidence of a direct bias by gender and/or race/ethnicity.

Direct Discrimination

Imagine yourself as a state legislator with numerous responsibilities.[1] Throughout the year you work with your fellow state legislators to research issues and pass laws that will best serve your state. You spend time in hearings to ensure that the state bureaucracy is correctly implementing the laws you have passed. If you live in a state with a citizen legislature, you likely also have a full-time job in the private sector to help support you and your family. You have to keep an active profile in the community so your constituents will know what you are doing and will reelect you. In addition to all this, you receive e-mails and letters from constituents seeking your help. In any given week you receive hundreds of e-mails regarding your legislative responsibilities.

Now imagine that you are up for reelection next month. While you are extremely busy in a normal week, during the campaign season you are stretched even further. In a normal week you do not have time to answer all the e-mails you receive; during campaign season, it is even harder. You have to prioritize your efforts. In that situation, how would you treat the following e-mail?

Dear Representative,

My name is Jake Mueller and I'm trying to figure out how to register to vote for the upcoming election. I heard that the voter registration deadline is soon.

Who should I call in order to register? Also, is there anything special I need to do when I register so that I can vote in future primary elections?

Thanks,
Jake Mueller

---

[1] Part of the material in this chapter is drawn from my 2011 article with David Broockman ("Do Politicians Racially Discriminate against Constituents? A Field Experiment on State Legislators." *American Journal of Political Science* 55 (3): 463–477). I wish to thank the *American Journal of Political Science* and the Midwest Political Science Association for allowing me to use that material here.

Do you take the time to respond to this e-mail? Would your answer change if the e-mail came instead from someone named DeShawn Jackson? What if the sender indicated that he wanted to vote in future Republican (or Democratic) primary elections?

Bias in Legislative Outputs

After elected officials learn constituents' opinions, they still have to decide how to act. Even when officials do not exhibit bias in how they process constituents' opinions, they can exhibit bias in how they act on those opinions when creating outputs.

In this chapter I test whether legislators exhibit a direct bias in a particular type of legislative output: helping constituents with their e-mail requests. Because the requests in the e-mails are held constant, these experiments allow us to directly measure the relative level of effort that legislators put into constituent requests from different groups and thus test whether legislators exhibit a direct bias in the outputs they produce.

Biases and Legislative Responsiveness

Politicians' personal biases are a factor that can affect their behavior when they produce outputs. I design experiments to measure this bias and differentiate it from the bias that occurs because of officials' strategic considerations.

Strategic discrimination occurs when public officials exhibit bias against a group because they expect to derive electoral benefits by doing so (Fenno 1978, 9; Bartels 1998). Because the likelihood that someone will vote for the incumbent is often determined by unobserved factors that are correlated with voters' descriptive characteristics, such as race, gender, and SES, legislators may use constituents' descriptive characteristics to determine whether to target them. In other words, representatives may engage in strategic discrimination because they believe that their efforts to help a given group are unlikely to change the likelihood that members of that group will turn out and vote for them.

For expositional purposes I adopt the terms *personal preference* and *strategic* to capture the dichotomy that I test. Further, I use the term *in-group, personal preference* to describe the situation that results when elected officials (and their offices) exhibit a personal (nonstrategic) bias in favor of constituents who are like them.

The term *personal preference* is itself quite generic and could be further delineated. For example, numerous studies have looked into whether discrimination occurs because people exhibit prejudice against the out-group or exhibit favoritism toward the in-group (e.g., Bobo and Zubrinsky 1996; Dawson 1994; Bobo 2001; Broockman 2013; see also the general review in Hutchings and Valentino 2004). These two motives are observationally equivalent for the outcomes observed as part of this study (the in-group does better than the out-group), and both fall under the rubric in-group, personal preference.

I do not delve further into how this type of discrimination bias could be broken down for two main reasons. First, the term *personal preference* travels better across the multiple constituent characteristics I study (race, gender, and SES). As discussed in Chapter 2, it is not clear that the same type of motives that drive racial bias apply to gender bias and vice versa. Our social networks, for example, are more segregated along racial and ethnic lines than they are along other characteristics (McPherson, Smith-Lovin, and Cook 2001). The term *personal preference* is flexible enough to apply to various types of motives while still emphasizing the personal nature of the motive (and differentiating it from strategic motivations).

Second, some of the most important policy debates regarding bias and institutional design do not depend on whether the bias is driven by in-group favoritism or out-group prejudice. If the group in power is exhibiting favoritism (whatever the motive), this raises concerns about protection for groups out of power. Debates over the exact motive for this type of bias can sometimes hinder policy debates by leading discussions away from the main point: are protections needed for those not in power?

Race and Personal Bias: Experiment 1

The hypothetical scenario presented at the beginning of the chapter is taken from an experiment a colleague and I conducted in order to test whether state legislators exhibit a personal preference against racial minorities (Butler and Broockman 2011). In the study, which was conducted in October 2008, legislators received an e-mail from either a putatively white constituent or a putatively black constituent. If legislators exhibit a personal preference against racial minorities, then we should see that legislators are more likely to respond to a request for help when it comes from a white constituent.

David Broockman and I (Butler and Broockman 2011) conducted our experiment in October 2008 on a sample of roughly forty-five hundred U.S. state legislators.[2] Each of these legislators was sent an e-mail asking for help with registering to vote. Box 6.1 provides the full text of the e-mail sent to state legislators; each received just one e-mail. We signaled the race of the sender by randomizing[3] whether the message was signed by and sent from an e-mail

---

[2] The sample was drawn from legislators in forty-four U.S. states who had e-mail addresses that were available online through state legislative websites in September 2008. Each legislator was contacted using the e-mail address listed on the state's official legislative website. After sending the e-mails, about 5 percent of them immediately bounced back as undeliverable because the addresses were no longer valid. For the analysis I limit the sample to the e-mails that were successfully sent.

[3] We also had three treatments that signaled something about the partisan preference of the e-mail sender. Crossing the race treatment with the partisanship treatments gives a total of

---

BOX 6.1. **E-mail Sent to State Legislators in the 2008 Race Study**

From: [*Treatment Name*]
To: [Legislator's E-mail Address]
Subject: A Question on Registering to Vote

Dear [**Representative/Senator**] [**Legislator's Last Name**],

My name is [*Treatment Name*] and I'm trying to figure out how to register to vote for the upcoming election. I heard that the voter registration deadline is soon.

Who should I call in order to register? Also, is there anything special I need to do when I register so that I can vote in future [*{blank}/**Democratic/Republican**]* primary elections?

Thanks,
[*Treatment Name*]

Notes: Items in bold were manipulated across e-mails. Items in italics were assigned randomly based on the treatment group.

---

account with the name Jake Mueller or the name DeShawn Jackson. Because we also identified each legislator's race and ethnicity,[4] we can also test whether legislators exhibit in-group, personal preference related to race when it comes to helping constituents.

Differentiating Personal Preferences from Strategic Discrimination

Either personal preferences or strategic discrimination could lead legislators to treat our two hypothetical constituents differently. Strategic discrimination could occur, for example, if legislators use a constituent's race to make inferences about his or her partisan preference. While whites have split their votes fairly evenly for candidates from the two parties over the past few decades, blacks have voted overwhelmingly for Democratic candidates. Thus, we might expect that legislators who receive an e-mail from DeShawn Jackson will infer

---

six treatments. We assigned legislators to treatment groups using block randomization by state, legislative chamber, political party, and whether the legislator was up for reelection. This method balances the number of legislators sharing these characteristics across treatment groups while allowing each observation to remain equally likely to be assigned to each of the treatment groups. To test the robustness of our randomization scheme, we tested for any differences among the other observables on which we did not block: the legislative district's total population, the racial composition of the district, the race of the legislator, and the Squire index of state legislative professionalism (Squire 2007). The results of our randomization check indicate that our randomization scheme was highly successful, $\chi^2 (52) = 30.03$, p = .9966.

[4] We used the directories created by the National Conference of Black State Legislators, the National Association of Latino Elected Officials, the Arab American Institute, the National Caucus of Native American State Legislators, and the UCLA Asian American Studies Center to identify each legislator's race and ethnicity.

that he will vote for Democratic candidates in the next election. Such considerations might lead white Republican legislators to be less responsive to blacks even if they do not hold a personal preference against blacks. To control for this form of strategic discrimination, we also randomized what the e-mail signaled about the constituent's partisan preferences (this randomization was orthogonal to the race treatment). In asking whether there was anything the senders needed to do to register in future primary elections, we randomized whether they asked about Democratic primary elections, asked about Republican primary elections, or did not specify a party (see Box 6.1).

Signaling the partisan preference of the e-mail sender allows us to see whether legislators are more responsive to copartisans and whether they continue to favor people like themselves even when they know the sender's partisan preference. If the bias is driven by legislators using constituents' race to make inferences about their partisan preferences, then the racial differences should disappear once partisanship is signaled. Thus, if white Republicans are more responsive to Jake than DeShawn only because they infer that DeShawn is more likely to be a Democrat, they should be equally responsive to Jake the Democrat and DeShawn the Democrat (or Jake the Republican and DeShawn the Republican). When the e-mail directly signals the sender's partisanship, the legislator no longer needs to use the putative constituent's race to infer what his partisanship is. By holding constant the partisan preference of the sender, we can see if the discrimination we observed was due to strategic partisan considerations and also determine if any residual discrimination remains that is not attributable to these considerations.

Why Not Ask Legislators about Discrimination Directly?

While interviews should continue to be an important way to learn about legislators (Fenno 1978; Kingdon 1981; Bianco 1994; Miler 2007, 2010), high levels of social desirability are likely to bias such interview responses. Such bias can also be correlated with expectations about one's party position. Paul Sniderman and Edward Carmines (1997) looked at support for affirmative action among white voters. When self-identified liberals are directly asked about their support for affirmative action, they show much more support than do self-identified conservatives. However, when Sniderman and Carmines use a list experiment to ask about individuals' attitudes toward affirmative action in a way that does not force any given individual to reveal his or her personal preference on the issue, they find that liberals and conservatives are equally dissatisfied with the policy. Instead of interviewing legislators, I directly measure whether their offices proactively show bias in their behavior, avoiding the need to rely on self-reports.

Why Not Look at Other Forms of Constituency Service Provision?

The audit study used here ensures that changes in demand for constituency service are not driving the results. Previous studies suggest that black legislators are more likely to include more racial content in their newsletters (Canon 1999) and locate their district offices in places with larger black populations (Grose 2011). However, these results do not indicate whether constituents are treated differently when the demand for service is held constant. Black legislators may have offices in black neighborhoods (or change the content of their newsletters) because descriptive representation leads to increased demand for constituency service among black constituents (see Grose 2011, 128).

As previous studies do not rule out the possibility that descriptive representation leads to a change in the demand for constituency services, an appropriate test of bias at the output stage of the representation process requires holding the constituent's request constant. The experimental design allows me to hold the demand side of the equation constant and test whether legislators exhibit a personal bias on the supply side by sending legislators similar requests from putative constituents of different races and ethnicities. In other words, I test whether legislators and staff show a preference for constituents who are descriptively similar to the legislators when holding constant the service that is requested.

Why Use Made Up Aliases Instead of Real Constituents?

Well-designed audit studies isolate, to the best extent possible, the degree to which the actors being studied respond to the characteristic of interest (in this case, the constituent's race). Isolating the impact of constituents' race means holding all other factors constant. Holding all other factors constant is important because researchers have criticized studies that use comparable minority and white actors to test for bias (Fix and Tuner 1998; Pager and Quillian 2005; Pager, Western, and Bonikowski 2009) because of the difficulty in identifying pairs of confederates who are comparable across all potentially relevant dimensions (Heckman and Siegelman 1992; Heckman 1998; cf. Pager 2007). These critics argue that the remaining differences in how the actors are treated may be driven by these other differences and not race.

More recent field experiments on labor market discrimination have overcome the problem of potential confounders by randomizing the names on resumes used to apply for jobs to signal the putative job candidate's race, gender, or religion (Bertrand and Mullainathan 2004; Adida, Laitin, and Valfort 2010). Because the researchers are not using real people, they can manipulate the information that the resumes convey (and hold this information constant!).

I use aliases in my constituency service field experiments because it allows me to manipulate the information provided in the e-mails and thus to avoid concerns that legislators might be responding to some other factor not held constant across treatments. It is possible to use real constituents for experiments. For example, Chris Karpowitz, Jeremy Pope, and I recruited approximately two hundred individuals to write and send letters to their state and federal legislators for a study we did (see Butler, Karpowitz, and Pope 2012). There are

TABLE 6.1. *Party Registration of Actual Individuals with Experimentally Manipulated Names*

	First Name DeShawn	Last Name Jackson	First Name Jake/Jacob	Last Name Mueller
Republican	9.7%	30.9%	44.2%	43.5%
Democrat	80.6%	63.0%	46.7%	45.7%
Other/Independent	9.7%	6.1%	9.1%	10.8%
Observations	72	8,249	2,282	538

Notes: Data are from the 2008 Kentucky voter file and show the party registration of actual individuals with the names of the aliases used in the study. The data indicate that the last name Jackson and the first name DeShawn are both strong signals of a Democratic partisan preference.

advantages to this approach but also important limitations – most siginficantly the inability to manipulate constituents' personal information. The ability to manipulate information about those who are asking for help allows us to design studies that increase our confidence that we are identifying a personal bias (and not a form of strategic discrimination).

Why the Aliases DeShawn Jackson and Jake Mueller?

We chose the first names Jake and DeShawn because Fryer and Levitt (2004) show that these names are among the most racially distinct. Among individuals named DeShawn, almost all are black; among individuals named Jake, almost all are white. Similarly, we chose the surnames Mueller and Jackson because data from the 2000 U.S. Census indicate that among common surnames these were, respectively, among those most strongly correlated with self-identification as white or black (Word et al. n.d.).

The partisan preferences of individuals with the names Jake Mueller and DeShawn Jackson also reflect the larger patterns of partisan support among whites and blacks in the United States as a whole. Table 6.1 shows the distribution of party registration among individuals with these names in an available voter file we had at the time of the study (Kentucky's). The last name Jackson and the first name DeShawn are both strong signals of a Democratic partisan preference: the ratio of people registered as Democrats compared to the number registered as Republicans is 2:1 among people with the last name Jackson and 8:1 among people with the first name DeShawn. In contrast, people with the first name Jake or Jacob and the last name Mueller are split evenly across the two parties. Given these patterns, legislators are likely to have a strong belief that DeShawn Jackson has a Democratic preference, but not have a strong prior belief about the partisan preferences of someone named Jake Mueller.

Why Send the E-mails the Month before the Election?

We sent the e-mails during the first weekend of October 2008 because several of the states' voter registration deadlines were the following week. We wanted to send the e-mails before these deadlines passed but also at a time when the legislators were busy with the campaign season so that they could potentially use the extra level of activity as an excuse to ignore the e-mails. This was apparently successful: even among legislators who ultimately replied, several noted the business of the campaign season as a reason for their lateness.

I am very sorry that I missed your email. I hope that you were able to find the registrar in your city or county and register. October 6th was the deadline for the Presidential election. You may still register but unfortunately you will not be able to vote on November 4th.
Again, my apologies for not seeing your correspondence sooner.

I am sorry I did not get this email sooner. The deadline was yesterday, I hope you had a chance to register.

A legislator in Alaska responded to the Jake alias as follows.

I apologize that your message arrived in the midst of my email account being bombarded with messages from around the world about Sarah Palin. In our efforts to clear these messages, I fear we overlooked your message.

Sending the e-mails a month before Election Day also ensured that strategic partisan considerations were highly salient for the legislators. Because we sent all the e-mails at the same time, the time between legislators receiving them and the voter registration deadline differed across states. As the partisan composition of legislatures also varies across states, any differences we observed between the parties might be the result of differences in how much time each group had to respond before the voter registration deadline. Figure 6.1 graphs, by party, the cumulative density by how many days before the voter registration deadline the legislators were sent the e-mail request. There are almost no differences between the parties. Republicans had an average of 13 days to respond to the e-mails before the voter registration deadlines in their states while Democrats had 13.4 days.

Is Partisanship the Only Important Potential Source of Strategic Discrimination?

Partisanship is an important source of strategic discrimination, but not the only source. Candidates care about how constituents vote and whether they turn out. If citizens do not vote, they cannot affect the outcome. Many models of political competition focus on both who citizens are likely to vote for and whether they will choose to vote at all (see Adams, Merrill, and Grofman 2005). Thus, we have reason to suspect that legislators might try to use information about constituents' race or ethnicity to make inferences about how likely they are to turn out to vote. Legislators also have incentives to worry about constituents' SES. A citizen's SES predicts how involved in politics he or she is and how able he or she is to make political donations (APSA Task Force 2004; see also Verba, Schlozman, and Brady 1995).

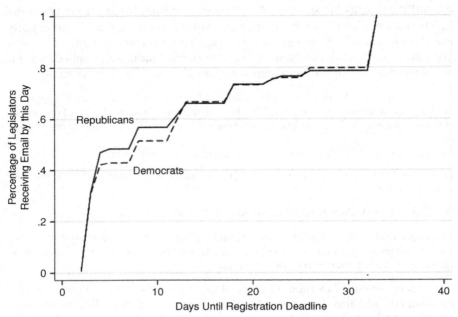

FIGURE 6.1. Differences between parties in time available to respond in the 2008 experiment. This figure gives the cumulative distribution by the legislators' partisanship of the number of days left before the registration deadline in their states at the time they received the e-mails. The solid (dashed) line gives the cumulative distribuion for Republicans (Democrats).

Another concern about the 2008 study is that the e-mails explicitly discussed primary elections. The legislators receiving those e-mails may have been worrying about the primary and not the general election when deciding how to respond. In safe districts, especially those with significant numbers of both black and white voters, legislators might use race to make inferences about how likely a voter is to support them in a primary election. White Democrats might worry that black voters might not support them in a primary, and minority Democrats might have similar concerns about white voters. More generally, even when an e-mail includes a lot of information, it is difficult to convince legislators that white and minority individuals will vote the same way in every election.

I ran a second constituency service field experiment in 2010 that dealt with all these issues by randomizing whether the e-mails included information about putative constituents' likelihood of turning out, their partisan preferences, and their likely SES. Most important, one of the treatments implies that the e-mail sender does not usually vote. When someone does not vote, most strategic concerns are taken off the table. Thus we can see whether legislators continue to exhibit an in-group, personal bias when other strategic concerns are not salient. For the 2010 study I also randomized whether the requests came from a putative constituent who was, based on their name, likely black, Latino, or non-Latino white.

Race, Ethnicity, and Personal Bias: Experiment 2

I conducted the second experiment on personal bias and race during the summer of 2010. I designed the experiment to look at the effect of descriptive representation on how black, Latino, and non-Latino white constituents are treated. State legislators were again the test subjects – over 6,700 of them, from all fifty states.

One of the advantages of studying representation at the state level is that there are a large number of minority legislators serving at that level. Researchers rarely study the behavior of minority legislators because they limit their analysis to Congress, where there are relatively few minority legislators. Because I study state legislators, I can test the proposition that white legislators discriminate in favor of whites and minority legislators discriminate in favor of minorities. Because I also wanted to look at bias and descriptive representation for blacks, Latinos, and non-Latino whites, I excluded from the sample legislators belonging to any other minority group.[5]

In the experiment I randomized the content of the e-mail and the name of the putative alias to signal race/ethnicity. Box 6.2 provides the text of the e-mail sent to state legislators in the sample. Rather than asking all the legislators the same question (as we did in the 2008 study), each legislator was randomly assigned request for basic information about such things as voting, government services, taxes, and business. A list of the questions appears in the Chapter 3 Appendix.

I also increased the number of aliases used for the 2010 studies, creating a total of 123 e-mail aliases: 35 black, 42 Latino, and 46 white.[6] In choosing the

[5] I identified which legislators were black or members of other minority groups (Latino, Arab American, Native American, and Asian American) by using, respectively, the directories created by the National Conference of Black State Legislators, the National Association of Latino Elected Officials, the Arab American Institute, the National Caucus of Native American State Legislators, and the UCLA Asian American Studies Center.

[6] The black aliases were Alaliyah Booker, Alexus Banks, Darius Joseph, Darnell Banks, Tyreke Washington, DeAndre Jefferson, Deja Jefferson, Deja Mosley, DeShawn Korsey, Dominique Mosley, Ebony Mosley, Ebony Washington, Jada Mosley, Jamal Gaines, Jamal Rivers, Jasmin Jefferson, Jasmine Joseph, Jazmine Jefferson, Jermaine Gaines, Keisha Rivers, Kiara Jackson, Latonya Rivers, Latoya Rivers, LaShawn Banks, LaShawn Washington, Precious Washington, Rasheed Gaines, Raven Korsey, Shanice Booker, Terrance Booker, Tremayne Joseph, Trevon Jackson, Tyrone Booker, Tyrone Joseph, and Xavier Jackson.

The Latino aliases were Alfonso Gonzalez, Beatriz Ibarra, Beatriz Martinez, Blanca Ramirez, Carlita Torres, Carlos Perez, Carlos Torres, Carmela Velazquez, Carmen Barajas, Carmen Lopez,

---

BOX 6.2. **E-mail Sent to State Legislators in the 2010 Race/Ethnicity Study**

From: [*Treatment Name*]
To: [Legislator's E-mail Address]
Subject:

Dear [Representative/Senator] [Legislator's Last Name],

[*{blank} / I usually don't vote, but I had a question. / Though I'm a {Democrat/ Republican} I haven't voted for a long time because I've been moving working construction. I'm writing now because I had a question.*]
    [Question randomly chosen from the Chapter 3 Appendix].

Sincerely,
[*Treatment Name*]

Notes: Items in bold were manipulated across e-mails. Items in italics were assigned randomly based on the treatment group. For the treatment signaling a partisan preference, we always signaled that the putative constituent was of the same party as the legislator.

---

aliases, I used information from previous studies and the U.S. Census (Fryer and Levitt 2004; Word et al. n.d.) to identify common first and last names for each racial or ethnic group I used as treatments. The treatment name was again found in both the e-mail address and the salutation of the message.[7]

For the roughly 6,000 non-Latino white legislators in the sample, I randomized whether they received an e-mail from an alias that was putatively black, putatively white, or putatively Latino. For the nearly 600 black legislators in the sample, I randomized whether they received an e-mail from a putatively white or putatively black individual. Finally, the roughly 200 Latino legislators in the sample each received two e-mails, one from a putatively white person and one from a putatively Latino person. I used these legislators twice

Carola Huerta, Carola Ibarra, Catalina Hernandez, Catalina Jaurez, Cesar Vazquez, Cesar Zavala, Dolores Ramirez, Dolores Sanchez, Edgar Sanchez, Edgar Zavala, Eduardo Lopez, Eduardo Torres, Enrique Huerta, Hernan Garcia, Javier Gonzalez, Jorge Cervantes, Jose Martinez, Jose Orozco, Jose Sanchez, Juan Barajas, Juan Hernandez, Luis Hernandez, Luis Vazquez, Magdalena Perez, Margarita Garcia, Margarita Velazquez, Maria Ramirez, Maria Rodriguez, Pedro Rodriguez, Rosa Orozco, Rosa Perez, and Teresa Jaurez.

    The white aliases were Abigail Smith, Allison Nelson, Amy Mueller, Anne Evans, Bradley Schwartz, Brett Clark, Caitlin Schneider, Carly Smith, Carrie King, Claire Schwartz, Cody Anderson, Cole Krueger, Colin Smith, Connor Schwartz, Dustin Nelson, Dylan Schwartz, Emily Schmidt, Emma Clark, Garrett Novak, Geoffrey Martin, Greg Adams, Hannah Phillips, Heather Martin, Holly Schroeder, Hunter Miller, Jack Evans, Jake Clark, Jay Allen, Jenna Anderson, Jill Smith, Katelyn Miller, Katherine Adams, Kathryn Evans, Katie Novak, Kristen Clark, Logan Allen, Luke Phillips, Madeline Haas, Matthew Anderson, Maxwell Haas, Molly Kruger, Sarah Miller, Scott King, Tanner Smith, Todd Mueller, and Wyatt Smith.
[7] Consistent with the claim that the names effectively signaled the ethnicity of the writer, one of the legislators responded to a putative Latino constituent in Spanish.

because I had a small sample and I wanted to get more power. I compared only how black and white legislators treat black and white constituents, and how Latino and white legislators treat Latino and white constituents. I did not test to see how minority legislators respond to constituents from other minority groups.

For the experiment I also varied the content of the e-mails by randomizing the first sentence or two in order to test whether legislators were engaging in strategic discrimination by using the constituents' race/ethnicity to infer politically relevant information.[8] If legislators were using race/ethnicity to infer this information about the constituent then when we include this information in the e-mail itself, the person responding would not need to use the constituent's race or ethnicity to make inferences. If the e-mail provided all the relevant information that legislators might try to infer from a constituent's race or ethnicity, we could assume that any residual differential treatment was attributable to these legislators' personal biases. I focused on the constituents' partisanship and their likelihood of turning out to vote because these two pieces of information were particularly relevant to legislators trying to win elections.

Because the 2008 study (see Box 6.1) tested the effect of partisanship alone on legislative responsiveness, the 2010 study looked at the effect of turnout behavior alone. The low turnout condition e-mail began with the sentence "I usually don't vote, but I had a question."

The 2010 study also included a treatment that tried to signal the putative constituent's partisan preference, likely turnout behavior, and other potentially politically relevant variables. The e-mails in the combined condition opened with "Though I'm a {Democrat/Republican} I haven't voted for a long time because I've been moving working construction. I'm writing now because I had a question." For this treatment I always signaled that the putative constituent was of the same party as the legislator. This treatment signaled that the constituent was a construction worker, to help control both for inferences about the constituent's SES (Fryer and Levitt 2004) and ability to make political donations and for the likelihood that the constituent was a longtime resident. This combined treatment was designed to give the relevant information that strategic legislators should care about most (and not to measure the separate effect of these different pieces of information). If legislators continued to exhibit racial or ethnic bias even after obtaining all the information, it could be considered strong evidence that personal preferences (not strategic considerations) were driving the bias.

Because of the small number of Latino legislators, I only used the control and combined content conditions with them. Each Latino legislator received one e-mail in the control condition and one e-mail in the combined condition.

---

[8] I block randomized (with blocks that consisted of the state, legislative chamber, and party of the legislator) both the question and the alias to minimize the possibility that legislators would become suspicious because they and their colleagues were receiving similar e-mails.

TABLE 6.2. *Overall Race and Responsiveness in 2008*

	Responded	Timely Response	Answered Question
White Alias	60.5%	57.8%	31.9%
Black Alias	55.3%	53.0%	31.4%
Difference	5.1*	4.8*	0.5
(Std. Error)	(2.5)	(2.5)	(2.3)
Observations	1,618	1,618	1,618

Notes: **Sig at the 0.01 level (one-tailed), *Sig at the 0.05 level (one-tailed). These results use only the legislators assigned to the control group. The percentages in the table give the percentage of legislators whose responses met the requirements for the measured outcome. The differences between the ways the non-Latino white alias and minority alias are treated are given in percentage points at the bottom of each section with the standard errors given in parentheses. These values are calculated so that positive values indicate a differential treatment in favor of the white alias and negative values a differential treatment in favor of the minority alias.

Finally, the e-mails themselves were sent over a two-week period in July; the order in which they were sent was also block randomized.

Results on Race and Personal Bias: The Control Group

For all of the experiments in this chapter I look at whether the legislator responded, whether it was a timely response (within two weeks), and whether the response answered the question.[9] I begin with overall response rates to white and black aliases from the 2008 study.[10] Table 6.2 shows these differences and the overall rates of reply for these two experimental groups. Legislators and their staff responded to 60.5 percent of the e-mails sent from the Jake alias but only 55.3 percent of those sent from the DeShawn alias, a statistically significant difference of 5.1 percentage points. Legislators are, overall, less responsive to minority constituents.

The lower responsiveness levels for black constituents can be traced to the racial composition of state legislators. Table 6.3 highlights this aspect of discrimination by breaking down the results of the experiments by the legislators'

---

[9] These last two outcomes are coded so those who do not provide a response that meets the criteria are grouped with those who do not respond at all. I make this comparison rather than comparing the quality of the responses across treatments among those who respond because the possibility of self-selection potentially biases any measures that only use the sample of those who respond (see the discussion in Angrist and Pischke 2009, 94–102).

[10] I only present the 2008 study because in the 2010 study the probability of receiving the different treatments was not equal for everyone in the sample. For example, the Latino treatment was only sent to Latino and non-Latino white constituents. In the 2008 study the probability of receiving the treatment was equal for the whole sample.

TABLE 6.3. *Testing the Effect of Descriptive Representation on Legislators'*
Responsiveness by Their Race/Ethnicity

(A) 2008 Race Study: Black and Non-Latino White Aliases

	Non-Latino White Legislators			Minority Legislators		
	Responded	Timely Response	Answered Question	Responded	Timely Response	Answered Question
White Alias	64.0%	61.2%	33.5%	33.3%	31.2%	19.4%
Black Alias	56.8%	54.4%	31.3%	45.8%	43.9%	31.8%
Difference	7.2**	6.8**	2.2	−12.5*	−12.7*	−12.4*
(Std. Error)	(2.6)	(2.6)	(2.5)	(5.1)	(6.9)	(6.2)
Observations	1,418	1,418	1,418	200	200	200

(B) 2010 Race Study: Black and White Aliases

	Non-Latino White Legislators			Black Legislators		
	Responded	Timely Response	Answered Question	Responded	Timely Response	Answered Question
White Alias	57.0%	51.4%	47.9%	28.0%	26.9%	22.6%
Black Alias	50.5%	45.4%	41.8%	31.0%	27%	24%
Difference	6.5**	5.9*	6.1*	−3.0	−0.1	−1.4
(Std. Error)	(2.7)	(2.8)	(2.7)	(6.6)	(6.4)	(6.1)
Observations	1,318	1,318	1,318	193	193	193

(C) 2010 Race Study: Latino and Non-Latino White Aliases

	Non-Latino White Legislators			Latino Legislators		
	Responded	Timely Response	Answered Question	Responded	Timely Response	Answered Question
White Alias	57.0%	51.4%	47.9%	29.6%	27.8%	23.2%
Latino Alias	49.2%	44.8%	37.2%	40.7%	35.2%	27.8%
Difference	7.8**	6.6**	10.7**	−11.1*	−7.4	−4.6
(Std. Error)	(2.7)	(2.7)	(2.7)	(6.5)	(6.3)	(5.9)
Observations	1,221	1,221	1,221	216	216	216

Notes: **Sig at the 0.01 level (one-tailed), *Sig at the 0.05 level (one-tailed). These results use only the legislators assigned to the control group. The percentages in the table give the percentage of legislators whose responses met the requirements for the measured outcome. The differences between the ways the non-Latino white alias and minority alias are treated are given in percentage points at the bottom of each section with the standard errors given in parentheses. These values are calculated so that positive values indicate a differential treatment in favor of the white alias and negative values a differential treatment in favor of the minority alias. Results are presented by the race/ethnicity of the legislators.

race. The results for non-Latino white legislators are presented on the left half
of the table and the results for minority legislators are presented on the right
half. The top portion of the table reports the results from the 2008 study and
shows that non-Latino white legislators responded to Jake Mueller (the white
alias) 64 percent of the time but responded to DeShawn Jackson (the black
alias) only 57 percent of the time. The white legislators were also more likely
to send a timely response to Jake than to DeShawn. Minority legislators exhibit
a bias in exactly the opposite direction. Minority legislators responded to 46
percent of the e-mails from DeShawn but only 33 percent of the emails from
Jake. Minority legislators were also more likely to respond in a timely manner
and with a response that actually answered the question when the e-mail came
from the putative black constituent.

Parts (B) and (C) of Table 6.3 provide the results from the 2010 study.
In general, the response rates in 2010 were lower than the response rates in
2008. In part this may reflect the differences in the questions that were asked. In
2008 legislators were asked for help in registering to vote. In 2010, by contrast,
legislators were asked a variety of questions dealing with campaigns, but also
with other aspects of state law (see the Chapter 3 Appendix). All politicians
know a lot about campaigns and all have vested interests in their outcomes,
so for these reasons it is not surprising that they were more responsive to the
question about registering to vote.

Even though response rates were lower overall, there is still a pattern of
differential responsiveness. While white legislators responded to 57 percent of
the responses from the putative white aliases, they only responded to roughly
50 percent of the e-mails from putative black and Latino constituents. This
means that, as in the 2008 study, white legislators were about seven percentage
points more likely to respond to the white constituents than to the minority constituents. They were also about six percentage points more likely to
respond in a timely manner and to answer the question in their response. These
differences are all statistically significant at conventional levels.

Because few studies look at how well Latinos are represented (cf. Griffin and
Newman 2008; see also the review in Swers and Rouse 2011), we know very
little about the level of discrimination that Latinos face relative to the discrimination faced by blacks. One of the important findings from the 2010 study
is that non-Latino white legislators engage in similar levels of discrimination
toward both Latino and black constituents.

The results also provide some evidence that minority legislators exhibit a
similar in-group bias that favors members of their group. The Latino legislators in the 2010 study responded to 41 percent of the e-mails from putative
Latino constituents, but only to 30 percent of the e-mails from putative white
constituents (an eleven-percentage-point difference!). The Latino legislators
were also about seven percentage points more likely to respond in a timely
manner.

Because relatively few studies have looked at the behavior of Latino public officials, the evidence for bias here provides important insights that challenge some of the existing work on Latino legislators. While Kerr and Miller (1997) argue that Latino legislators vote differently than other legislators, and give Latinos better substantive representation, most other studies conclude that Latino legislators do not exhibit distinctive voting patterns when controlling for other relevant factors, such as the percentage of Latino constituents in the district (Welch and Hibbing 1984; Hero and Tolbert 1995; Santos and Huerta 2001). In the 2010 study I find that Latino legislators are more responsive to their Latino constituents' e-mails.

The balance of the evidence shows that legislators from all three groups – non-Latino whites, Latinos, and blacks – show favoritism toward members of their own group. Indeed, with the exception of the black legislators in the 2010 study, the legislators were all more responsive, at statistically significant levels, to constituents who were descriptively like themselves. The non-Latino white legislators were more responsive to non-Latino white constituents and the minority legislators were more responsive to the minority constituents. Even the black legislators in the 2010 study were more responsive to the black alias (though not at statistically significant levels).

Does Partisanship Explain In-Group Favoritism by Race/Ethnicity?

Descriptive representation is not necessarily the sole determinant of how responsive politicians are to their constituents. One possibility is that legislators' political partisanship, not their race or ethnicity, is driving their behavior. Lublin (1997) argues that black and white legislators vote differently, but the racial differences are small relative to the difference between Democrats and Republicans. Because minority legislators are in practice disproportionately Democrats, a Democratic bias toward minority constituents could explain the behavior of minority legislators. Similarly, if Republicans showed more of a bias for non-Latino white constituents than Democrats showed for minority constituents, this might explain the behavior of non-Latino white legislators.

Ruling out the possibility that the observed benefits associated with descriptive representation are driven by legislators' partisanship is important because it has implications for debates about racial redistricting. If legislators' race is the key determinant of substantive representation, then minority voters are likely to be better served by having majority-minority districts that are likely to elect a minority candidate because minorities represent 60 or more percent of the district's population. However, if legislators' partisanship is the key determinant of substantive representation for minority voters, then minority voters might be better off in districts where they only represent a key swing constituency (say 25 percent of the voters). They are unlikely to elect minority representatives, but they are likely to elect Democrats. Thus knowing whether legislators' partisanship or race is the key determinant of substantive representation for minorities affects the type of redistricting that best benefits minorities. In turn this question depends on knowing whether white Democrats are a good substitute for minority Democrats. In other words, does legislators' partisanship or race explain the observed patterns of in-group favoritism?

The Behavior of Non-Latino White Legislators in the Control Condition

Table 6.4 shows the results for non-Latino white legislators by partisanship for the control content treatments in both the 2008 and 2010 studies. The left side of the table shows the results for non-Latino white Republicans and the right side the results for non-Latino white Democrats. In all three studies there is roughly an equal number of non-Latino white Republicans and Democrats. Combining all white legislators, we found that they were six to eight percentage points more responsive to the non-Latino white alias than the minority alias for all three outcomes. Dividing the sample by partisanship, the pattern holds for both Republicans and Democrats. Because I have divided the sample in half, the differences are not always statistically significant, but the pattern is clear: white legislators from both parties are five to eight percentage points more responsive to e-mails from white constituents than to similar e-mails from minority constituents. Similarly, white legislators from both parties are more likely to respond to white constituents in a timely manner and to answer the constituent's question.

The Behavior of Minority Legislators in the Control Condition

Table 6.5 shows the results when the sample is limited to minority Democratic legislators.[11] The results for the Democratic minority legislators reinforce the same conclusion as before: minority Democrats are more responsive to e-mails from minority constituents. Partisanship is not driving the results. Legislators of both parties favor people from their own racial or ethnic groups. Thus, when it comes to substantive representation on constituency casework, white Democrats are not a substitute for minority representatives.

Can Strategic Discrimination Explain In-Group Favoritism by Race/Ethnicity?

Minority constituents vote disproportionately for Democratic candidates. It is possible that non-Latino white Republicans discriminate against minority constituents because they do not want to invest time in constituents who, because of their partisan preferences, are unlikely to vote Republican. The same logic might explain why minority Democrats are less responsive to white

---

[11] I do not present the results for Republican minority legislators because there are not enough observations.

TABLE 6.4. *Results for Responsiveness by Partisanship for Non-Latino White Legislators*

(A) 2008 Race Study: Black and Non-Latino White Aliases

	Non-Latino White Republicans			Non-Latino White Democrats		
	Responded	Timely Response	Answered Question	Responded	Timely Response	Answered Question
White Alias	66.9%	64.0%	34.6%	61.2%	58.4%	32.5%
Black Alias	59.3%	56.4%	29.3%	54.3%	52.3%	33.3%
Difference	7.6*	7.6*	5.2	6.8*	6.1	−0.8
(Std. Error)	(3.6)	(3.7)	(3.5)	(3.7)	(3.7)	(3.5)
Observations	707	707	707	711	711	711

(B) 2010 Race Study: Black and White Aliases

	Non-Latino White Republicans			Non-Latino White Democrats		
	Responded	Timely Response	Answered Question	Responded	Timely Response	Answered Question
White Alias	59.2%	53.0%	50.9%	54.7%	49.7%	44.7%
Black Alias	53.9%	48.5%	44.1%	46.9%	42.2%	39.4%
Difference	5.3	4.4	6.8*	7.8*	7.5*	5.3
(Std. Error)	(3.8)	(3.8)	(3.8)	(3.9)	(3.9)	(3.9)
Observations	674	674	674	644	644	644

(C) 2010 Race Study: Latino and Non-Latino White Aliases

	Non-Latino White Republicans			Non-Latino White Democrats		
	Responded	Timely Response	Answered Question	Responded	Timely Response	Answered Question
White Alias	59.2%	53.0%	50.9%	54.7%	49.7%	44.7%
Latino Alias	51.8%	47.3%	37.8%	46.5%	42.2%	36.6%
Difference	7.4*	5.6	13.1**	8.2*	7.5*	8.1*
(Std. Error)	(3.8)	(3.9)	(3.8)	(3.9)	(3.9)	(3.9)
Observations	674	674	674	647	647	647

Notes: **Sig at the 0.01 level (one-tailed), *Sig at the 0.05 level (one-tailed). These results use only the legislators assigned to the control group. The percentages in the table give the percentage of legislators whose responses met the requirements for the measured outcome. The differences between the ways the non-Latino white alias and minority alias are treated are given in percentage points at the bottom of each section with the standard errors given in parentheses. These values are calculated so that positive values indicate a differential treatment in favor of the white alias and negative values a differential treatment in favor of the minority alias. Results are presented by the partisanship of the non-Latino white legislators in the sample.

constituents. They know that non-Latino white constituents are less likely to vote for them than a minority constituent is. In other words, non-Latino white Republicans and minority Democrats might be favoring constituents from their own group for strategic partisan reasons, not because they have a

TABLE 6.5. *Results for Responsiveness by Partisanship for Minority Democratic Legislators*

	Responded	Timely Response	Answered Question
(A) 2008 Race Study: Black and White Aliases – Minority Democrats			
White Alias	29.4%	27.1%	17.7%
Black Alias	45.9%	43.9%	31.6%
Difference	−16.5*	−16.8**	−14.0*
(Std. Error)	(7.1)	(7.0)	(6.4)
Observations	183	183	183
(B) 2010 Race Study: Black and White Aliases – Black Democrats			
White Alias	27.2%	27.2%	21.7%
Black Alias	31.3%	27.3%	24.2%
Difference	−4.1	−0.1	−2.5
(Std. Error)	(6.6)	(6.5)	(6.1)
Observations	191	191	191
(C) 2010 Race/Ethnicity Study: White and Latino Aliases – Latino Democrats			
White Alias	29.8%	27.7%	23.4%
Latino Alias	40.5%	34.8%	29.2%
Difference	−10.7	−7.2	−5.8
(Std. Error)	(7.0)	(6.9)	(6.5)
Observations	183	183	183

Notes: **Sig at the 0.01 level (one-tailed), *Sig at the 0.05 level (one-tailed). These results use only the legislators assigned to the control group. The percentages in the table give the percentage of legislators whose responses met the requirements for the measured outcome. The differences between the ways the non-Latino white alias and minority alias are treated are given in percentage points at the bottom of each section with the standard errors given in parentheses. These values are calculated so that positive values indicate a differential treatment in favor of the white alias and negative values a differential treatment in favor of the minority alias. Results are presented by the partisanship of the minority legislators in the sample.

personal preference for constituents who are similar to themselves. In addition to worrying about constituents' partisanship, politicians have incentives to care about whether a constituent votes. Only when constituents vote can they affect the outcome. The text of the legislators' responses showed that they were sensitive to these types of strategic considerations. For example:

Thank you for your email informing me you are a Democrat and asking for information about starting a new company...

Thanks for being a Republican and hope you vote in the future....

As far as political party, once you declare yourself a Democrat or Republican, you can vote in that party's next primary in 2010. You could even register as one party and switch at the next primary if you wanted to.

Only Independents are prevented from voting in primaries.

I'm excited that you want to register as a Democrat. There's not many of us in this part of the state.

Also, Representative [Redacted] would like to extend an invitation for you to come and spend the day here at the Capitol and we can show you around and he can also take you on the House Floor during Session. Make sure you vote this year! It is probably one of the most important election years in some time. If you know that you will be out of town, you can do an early absentee vote.

Thanks for the e-mail. I'm glad you're taking an interest in politics, and voicing your input through voting! For your first time voting you will need...

I am retiring... so you can't vote for me if you decide to vote, but you can vote for the Democrat who wins in the primary if you so desire!

Please vote this year. We need your vote more than ever.

The two experiments were designed to test whether, in line with these types of sentiments, the white Republican and minority Democratic legislators were engaging in strategic discrimination by simply using the race/ethnicity of the constituent to give a preference to likely copartisans or likely voters. In the 2008 study, David Broockman and I randomized whether the e-mail included information about the sender's partisan preference (see Box 6.1). In the 2010 study I used a combined content treatment to signal that the constituent identified with the legislator's party (see Box 6.2) and a treatment indicating that the constituent had not voted frequently in past elections. With these manipulations, we can see whether legislators are using race or ethnicity to infer an individual's likelihood of voting or partisan preference – that is, whether they are engaging in strategic discrimination. If the discrimination we observed among non-Latino white Republicans and minority Democrats is strategic in nature, then it should disappear when the e-mail includes the additional information because the sender's race or ethnicity would then convey no additional information about partisanship or the likelihood of turning out to vote.

For these tests I focus only on the responded outcome to conserve space; the results are similar for the other outcomes. I begin by testing whether legislators noticed and acted on the content treatments. It is possible that legislators and their staff may have missed the additional information, especially in the 2008 experiment, in which the partisan signal was part of the second paragraph of the e-mail (see Box 6.1). Table 6.6 shows the differences in how legislators responded to the content treatments.

Legislators' Response to the Partisan Preferences of the Putative Constituents

The top half of Table 6.6 shows that the legislators noticed and reacted to the partisanship signal. Democrats responded to 56 percent of the writers who expressed an interest in the Democratic primary but to only 51 percent of those

TABLE 6.6. *Effect of the Content Treatments on Responsiveness*

(A) 2008 Race Study

	Democrats	Republicans
Republican Primary	51.2%	60.6%
Democratic Primary	56.3%	56.3%
Difference	−5.1*	4.3*
(Std. Error)	(2.4)	(2.6)
N	1,795	1,446

(B) 2010 Race/Ethnicity Study

	All Legislators
Control Treatment	48.8%
Low Turnout Treatment	52.5%
Combined Treatment	50.4%
Difference: Low Turnout – Control	3.7**
(Std. Error)	(1.5)
Difference: Combined – Control	1.6
(Std. Error)	(1.4)
N	6,951

Notes: **Sig at the 0.01 level (one-tailed), *Sig at the 0.05 level (one-tailed). This measures whether the content treatments in the 2008 and 2010 studies had any effect on legislators' responsiveness (i.e., the dependent variable in all of the analyses is whether the legislator *responded*). The percentages in the table give the percentage of legislators whose responses met the requirements for the measured outcome. The differences between how legislators responded to the different treatments are given at the bottom of each section in percentage point terms with the associated standard error given in parentheses.

who were interested in learning more about the Republican primary. Republicans responded to 60 percent of the e-mails that asked about the Republican primary but to only 56 percent of those that asked about the Democratic primary. Thus members of both parties were about five percentage points more responsive to writers who expressed an interest in their party's primary. Consistent with their strategic interests, legislators showed a clear preference for fellow partisans.

Legislators' Response to the Past Turnout Behavior of the Putative Constituents

The bottom half of Table 6.6 gives the results for the way legislators responded to the content treatments in the 2010 race/ethnicity study. There were three content treatments: the control treatment, the low turnout treatment, and the combined treatment (see Box 6.2). Because the 2008 study tested the effect of partisanship alone on legislative responsiveness, the 2010 study included a treatment to look at the effect of one's likely turnout behavior alone. The 2010 study also included a combined treatment that gave information about constituents' partisan preference, their likely turnout behavior, their SES, and the fact that they moved frequently.

The results at the bottom of Table 6.6 show that legislators who received e-mails from people who said they "usually don't vote" were nearly four percentage points more likely – a statistically significant difference – to send a response than were the legislators in the control condition who received no additional information about the putative constituent. This was a surprising result; my expectation when designing the experiment was that the low turnout treatment condition would receive fewer responses. I looked at the responses that legislators sent to these e-mails to see what might be driving the results. Many of the legislators who received this treatment directly responded to the reference about putative constituents' turnout behavior, encouraging them to participate. Here are some example snippets:

Thanks again for writing and I encourage you to exercise your right and vote.

I am sorry to hear that you usually don't vote. I hope you will consider voting at the next scheduled election as it is an important part of the process.

I certainly would encourage you to vote!

Sorry to learn of your decision not to vote. . . . I feel it is every U.S. citizen's right to vote have have their voice heard in our government.

I wish you would vote.

BTW, it's not too late to register to vote for the general election in November.

An equal number of legislators made more involved appeals to the writer to vote. Some invoked civic duty, but more often their appeals dealt directly with the outcome of the election. These legislators discussed the possibility that the race would be close or emphasized the importance of choosing the best candidates.

I hope you will consider voting in the November election. Everyone's vote is important and sometimes races can be won by only a few votes.

I'm sad to learn you do not vote. It makes a difference. In my first election, I won . . . by only [a small number of] votes. Every vote DOES count.

First of all, I strongly encourage you to register and vote. Our country, and our State, are in deep trouble and we need every citizen to be involved.

If you don't know enough about the process, or don't have any idea what each candidate stands for, I will be happy to give you my opinion, and if you want me to, I will help you find others that can give you a differing viewpoint so you can compare.

Some of these races this year are very important. And some will be decided by just a handful of votes. Very often, one vote DOES matter!

Of course, I really strongly think that you should vote. This is particularly true if you take the time to examine how public officials approach their campaigns and their jobs. You should vote for the ones that do better than others (or vote against those that do worse).

In light of statements like these, legislators may have been more likely to respond to the low turnout condition because they assumed that citizens who do not vote are also unlikely to have strong preexisting attachments (Fiorina 1981) and may have hoped to win these voters over by serving them. Further, these types of constituents are also likely to be persons who might turn out to vote. Constituents who have exhibited enough political efficacy to write to their legislator are also likely to be of the type that engages in other political activities (Verba, Schlozman, and Brady 1995). In retrospect the treatment regarding not voting may have been a signal to legislators that the writer was likely to become a participatory citizen. Either way, legislators noticed and responded to this content in the e-mail.

Legislators assigned to the combined treatment were 1.5 percentage points more likely to respond to the e-mail they received than those in the control group, but this difference was not statistically significant. One likely reason that this treatment had no effect on legislative responsiveness is that the combined treatment provided several different pieces of information, some of which worked in opposite directions. Turnout and partisanship signals should have increased responsiveness, but moving frequently should have made legislators less excited about investing time in helping a constituent. Again, the purpose of the combined treatment is not to measure the effect of these different pieces of information but to see if we continue to find racial or ethnic bias after signaling the relevant information that strategic legislators should care most about.

Do White Republicans Use Race/Ethnicity to Engage in Strategic Discrimination?

Does the level of bias disappear when this additional information is conveyed? Again, the focus is on non-Latino white Republicans and minority Democrats because these legislators should be most likely to use constituents' race or ethnicity to engage in strategic partisan discrimination. Table 6.7 shows the results by treatment condition for the non-Latino white Republicans.

In each section of Table 6.7, I present the control condition in the first column. If legislators are engaging in strategic discrimination by using constituents' race or ethnicity to infer the political information we test for, then we should observe that the level of discrimination under the control condition disappears for the other content treatments. The top section of the table shows these results for the black and white aliases in the 2008 study.

In the control condition, when no additional information is given about the constituents' partisan preferences, the non-Latino white legislators are 7.6 percentage points more responsive to the white alias than to the black alias. When information about the constituent's partisan preference is signaled, this effect decreases, but only a little. The non-Latino white legislators continue to be 5.3 percentage points more responsive to the white alias. Although a difference in differences indicates that about 2.3 percentage points, or about 30 percent of

TABLE 6.7. *Is There Evidence of Strategic Discrimination by White Republicans?*

(A) 2008 Study: Black and Non-Latino White Aliases – White Republicans

	No Party	Republican	Democrat	Party Differential	
White Alias	66.9%	62.5%	59.5%	3.0	Combined
				(3.7)	3.7 (2.6)
Black Alias	59.3%	57.9%	53.5%	4.4	
				(3.7)	
Difference	7.6*	4.6	5.9		
(Std. Err)	(3.6)	(3.7)	(3.7)		
Observations	707	706	701		
		5.3* (2.6)			
		Combined Effect			

(B) 2010 Study: Black and Non-Latino White Aliases – White Republicans

	Control	Low Turnout	Combined
White Alias	59.2%	58.7%	59.0%
Black Alias	53.9%	49.3%	51.8%
Difference	5.3	9.4**	7.2*
(Std. Err)	(3.8)	(3.8)	(3.8)
Observations	674	671	674

(C) 2010 Study: Latino and Non-Latino White Aliases – White Republicans

	Control	Low Turnout	Combined
White Alias	59.2%	58.6%	58.9%
Latino Alias	51.8%	53.1%	50.1%
Difference	7.4*	5.5	8.8*
(Std. Err)	(3.8)	(3.8)	(3.8)
Observations	674	671	675

Notes: **Sig. at the 0.01 level (one-tailed), *Sig. at the 0.05 level (one-tailed). For each section, the first column supplies the response rates for the control group when no additional information is signaled. The second and third columns present the results when additional information is given (see Boxes 6.1 and 6.2). The differences between the ways the non-Latino white alias and minority alias are treated are given in percentage points at the bottom of each section with the standard errors given in parentheses. These values are calculated so that positive values indicate a differential treatment in favor of the white alias and negative values a differential treatment in favor of the minority alias. In the top section (the 2008 experiment), the second to last column in each section gives the difference between the response rates between the Republican and Democratic partisan signals for that particular alias, while the last column pools the party differential for both the black and white aliases. Positive values in these columns indicate differential treatment in favor of the Republican signal while negative values indicate differential treatment in favor of the Democratic signal.

the original effect, may be due to strategic partisan considerations, it is not statistically significant. Thus, while there is evidence that strategic considerations regarding voters' perceived partisanship might partially motivate the observed patterns of discrimination, there remain significant levels of discrimination that cannot be explained by strategic responses alone.

The results for the 2010 study are even more striking. Under the control condition, white Republican legislators are more responsive to non-Latino white constituents than they are to both black and Latino constituents. Further, under the combined treatment condition, the level of differential treatment increases. Again, the differences in differences are not statistically significant, but the favoritism exhibited toward the white alias strongly suggests that the racial bias non-Latino white legislators show for white constituents is not the result of the strategic considerations we experimentally manipulated.[12]

Do Minority Democrats Use Race/Ethnicity to Engage in Strategic Discrimination?

Table 6.8 presents evidence for whether minority Democrats are engaging in strategic discrimination. As with the white legislators, the level of differential treatment in the 2008 study decreases when constituents signal their partisan preference. Minority Democrats under the control condition are 16.5 percentage points more likely to respond to the black alias than to the white alias. The number is cut in half when constituents signal their partisan preference, suggesting that there may be some evidence that legislators use race to make inferences about constituents' preferences. However, the bias toward black constituents continues to be quite large – a difference of nearly 8 percentage points (though because of the small sample, it is no longer statistically significant). While there is again evidence that partisan considerations may be driving some of the bias in favor of the black alias, it cannot explain all of it.

The results from the 2010 study are similar. Under the control condition minority legislators are more responsive to minority constituents. When the additional information is signaled, they continue to show a preference for minority constituents. The most surprising result is for black legislators in the 2010 study: under the control condition they are 4 percentage points more responsive to the black alias than to the white alias. However, when the text of the e-mail signals that the constituent usually does not vote, the level of bias nearly triples to 11.5 percentage points, a difference that is statistically

---

[12] When voters imply that they are unlikely to vote – as the e-mail in the combined treatment suggests – many of the other strategic considerations that legislators and their offices might consider are taken off the table. When people do not vote, legislators do not need to influence their vote. That the observed level of discrimination remains high even when constituents imply they are unlikely to vote provides strong evidence that non-Latino white legislators favor non-Latino white constituents.

TABLE 6.8. *Is There Evidence of Strategic Discrimination by Minority Democrats?*

(A) 2008 Study: Black and Non-Latino White Aliases – Minority Democrats

	No Party	Republican	Democrat	Party Differential	
Anglo Alias	29.4%	25.3%	38.9%	−13.6*	Combined
				(6.7)	− 15.3** (5.1)
Black Alias	45.9%	31.4%	48.7%	−17.3*	
				(7.6)	
Difference	−16.5*	−6.1	−9.8		
(Std. Err)	(7.1)	(6.6)	(7.7)		
Observations	183	185	166		
		−7.8 (5.1)			
		Combined Effect			

(B) 2010 Study: Black and Non-Latino White Aliases – Black Democrats

	Control	Low Turnout	Combined
Anglo Alias	27.2%	25.2%	35.8%
Black Alias	31.3%	36.7%	39.8%
Difference	−4.1	−11.5*	−4.0
(Std. Err)	(6.6)	(6.7)	(7.1)
Observations	191	189	188

(C) 2010 Study: Latino and Non-Latino White Aliases – Latino Democrats

	Control	Low Turnout	Combined
Anglo Alias	29.7%	N/A	38.1%
Latino Alias	40.4%	N/A	44.3%
Difference	−10.7	N/A	−6.2
(Std. Err)	(7.0)		(7.3)
Observations	183		185

Notes: **Sig. at the 0.01 level (one-tailed), *Sig. at the 0.05 level (one-tailed). For each section, the first column supplies the response rates for the control group when no additional information is signaled. The second and third columns present the results when additional information is given (see Boxes 6.1 and 6.2). The differences between the ways the non-Latino white alias and minority alias are treated are given in percentage points at the bottom of each section with the standard errors given in parentheses. These values are calculated so that positive values indicate a differential treatment in favor of the white alias and negative values a differential treatment in favor of the minority alias. In the top section (the 2008 experiment), the second to last column in each section gives the difference between the response rates between the Republican and Democratic partisan signals for that particular alias, while the last column pools the party differential for both the black and white aliases. Positive values in these columns indicate differential treatment in favor of the Republican signal while negative values indicate differential treatment in favor of the Democratic signal.

significant at the 0.05 level. When they have information about constituents' likelihood of turning out to vote, they actually exhibit more bias in favor of their black constituents. This suggests that black legislators may be inferring that white constituents are more likely to vote. Black legislators in this case might be engaging in strategic discrimination that actually offsets the favoritism that arises from their personal preferences.[13]

Overall the results are quite clear: legislators are more responsive to constituents who share their race or ethnicity for reasons that extend beyond the strategic considerations tested here.

Do Legislators Exhibit a Personal Bias Related to Gender?

We can test whether legislators favor constituents who are of their gender because in the 2010 race study I also randomized whether each e-mail was sent by a putative male or female alias (see note 6 for the aliases used).

Table 6.9 breaks the results down by legislators' gender and partisanship. Male legislators from both parties treat the requests from their male and female constituents equally well. Male Republicans were only 1.6 percentage points, and male Democrats only half a percentage point, more likely to respond to an e-mail from a putative male constituent than to an e-mail from a putative female constituent. These results are substantively small and statistically insignificant. The results were the same for the other outcomes I measured. Male legislators do not exhibit any significant bias based on the gender of their constituents.

Nor is there evidence that female legislators favor female constituents. Female Republicans were 2.3 percentage points, and female Democrats 4.1 percentage points, more likely to respond to an e-mail from a putative male constituent than to an e-mail from a putative female constituent. These differences are larger than the differences that male legislators exhibit but smaller than the differences for race/ethnicity (i.e., 6 to 12 percentage points; see Table 6.3), and they are statistically insignificant. Perhaps most importantly, the differences go in an unexpected direction: female legislators were more responsive to their male constituents, though not at statistically significant levels.

With every study, there is a question of whether the results are applicable under other circumstances. It is worth pointing out that the gender results come from the same sample that exhibited an in-group, personal bias toward constituents from their racial or ethnic group (see the 2010 results in Tables 6.2–6.7). Given that these legislative offices exhibit personal biases in other ways, there is no reason to believe that the lack of bias related to gender occurs by chance. The evidence strongly suggests that legislators and their staff do not exhibit an in-group, personal bias related to gender.[14]

---

[13] If this interpretation is correct, it suggests that black legislators' favoritism is electorally constrained. They want to exhibit greater favoritism toward blacks, but they know that white voters are a significant part of the electorate that turns out to vote. To win they know they have to keep the electorate that votes, including white voters, happy.

[14] The results are quite similar when broken down by the putative race or ethnicity of the e-mail sender: the differences are statistically insignificant and in the few cases in which the magnitude rises over four percentage points, the effect goes in the wrong direction (i.e., women legislators are more responsive to men and vice versa).

TABLE 6.9. *Results for Responsiveness by Partisanship and Gender (2010 Study)*

	Male Republicans			Male Democrats		
	Respond	Timely Response	Answered Question	Respond	Timely Response	Answered Question
Female Alias	52.4%	50.4%	41.2%	48.3%	46.3%	39.4%
Male Alias	54.1%	51.9%	42.9%	48.8%	46.4%	38.9%
Difference	−1.6	−1.5	−1.7	−0.5	−0.1	0.5
(Std. Error)	(2.0)	(2.0)	(2.0)	(2.1)	(2.1)	(2.0)
Observations	2,556	2,556	2,556	2,368	2,368	2,368
	Female Republicans			Female Democrats		
	Respond	Timely Response	Answered Question	Respond	Timely Response	Answered Question
Female Alias	57.2%	53.2%	45.5%	47.9%	46.2%	39.9%
Male Alias	59.5%	56.0%	48.3%	52.0%	49.2%	43.2%
Difference	−2.3)	−2.8	−2.8	−4.1)	−3.0)	−3.3
(Std. Error)	(4.5)	(4.6)	(4.6)	(3.0)	(3.0)	(3.0)
Observations	481	481	481	1,110	1,110	1,110

Notes: **Sig at the 0.01 level (one-tailed), *Sig at the 0.05 level (one-tailed). The percentages in the table give the percentage of legislators whose responses met the requirements for the measured outcome. The differences between the ways the female alias and male alias are treated are given in percentage points at the bottom of each section with the standard errors given in parentheses. These values are calculated so that positive values indicate a differential treatment in favor of the female alias and negative values a differential treatment in favor of the male alias. Results are presented by the partisanship and gender of legislators in the sample.

Discussion

The experiments show that state legislators are more responsive to constituents from their racial or ethnic group, a result that holds for whites, blacks, and Latinos. These differences in responsiveness hold across parties and cannot be explained by legislators using constituents' race or ethnicity to infer their partisan preferences, their likelihood of turning out to vote, or their SES. Instead, legislators' personal biases lead them to be more responsive to constituents of their own race/ethnicity.

In contrast, there is no evidence that legislators exhibit an in-group, personal preference related to gender or SES. In Chapter 5, I presented evidence that a constituent's SES does not affect legislative responsiveness. In this chapter, I showed that a constituent's gender did not affect legislators' responsivness. Male and female legislators were no more likely to respond to constituents of the same gender as themselves. If anything, female legislaors seemed slightly more responsive to male constituents.

The lack of bias related to gender and SES only highlights the importance of the results related to race. Representation breaks down for racial minorities at the output stage (and for low-SES voters at the input stage). In the concluding chapter I discuss the significance of finding no gender-related bias.

Strategic Legislators

While I have shown that legislators are biased in favor of members of their own race, I have also shown that they are strategic. In the 2008 study David Broockman and I found that both Republicans and Democrats were more likely to respond to an e-mail from someone who indicated they intended to vote in future primary elections of the legislator's party. This comports with theoretical expectations that legislators care about catering to copartisans who might be part of their base; it is simply easier to appeal to fellow copartisans than it is to convert people with strong partisan attachments to the opposition party.

I also found evidence that legislators are sensitive to a constituent's previous turnout behavior. Unexpectedly, I found that telling legislators the writer "usually don't vote" actually increased the likelihood that they would respond. One possible explanation is that legislators and their offices assumed these citizens were less likely to have preexisting attachments and thus would be easier to win over (Fiorina 1981). Alternatively, these voters might be easier to win over simply because they have less information. This result deserves further exploration.

Race, Ethnicity, Party, and Public Policies

Even controlling for strategic considerations, the results show that all legislators exhibit bias that favors their racial in-group. The results from the 2010 study show that the bias in favor of one's copartisans is comparable in size to the bias in favor of constituents from one's racial in-group. These results are particularly stark because the experiments hold everything constant. In practice, racial groups differ in the extent to which they engage in politics. Groups might receive less attention because they participate less, but those biases occur after accounting for the underlying bias that groups exhibit in favor of constituents from their racial in-group.

One important finding is that this result applies to *both* non-Latino white legislators and minority legislators. Research typically only focuses on the behavior of white legislators and so has missed these patterns. To be clear, we have done nothing that looks at the motives behind the observed patterns of bias. It is possible that these groups' behavior is influenced by different motives: linked fate, in-group favoritism, and/or out-group prejudice are all potential culprits (e.g., Dawson 1994; Bobo and Zubrinsky 1996; Mendelberg 2001). Still, it is important to note that all groups exhibit a bias in favor of their own group.

Of course this does not necessarily mean that we should be equally concerned about the bias that these different groups of legislators exhibit. When groups hold power their bias is more likely to shape policy outcomes. While not excusing the bias that exists among groups out of power, it is important to acknowledge the power dynamics that exist and put in protections that prevent groups in power from hurting the interests of out-groups.

The need to protect groups out of power applies to both the partisan and racial biases we have uncovered. Thus, when Republicans control government, there are concerns about the interests of Democratic constituents, and vice versa for Republicans when Democrats are in control. However because parties, at least in recent decades, regularly take turns in power, this partisan bias is less concerning than racial bias.

Because most legislators in the United States are white, the net effect of their personal bias is that white constituents are favored. Given this situation, what can be done to protect the interests of racial minorities?

The Voting Rights Act

In June 2013 the Supreme Court sparked further discussion on this topic when it struck down section 4 of the Voting Rights Act (VRA). This decision raised questions about the protection of minority voters because the VRA has been successful in protecting minority voters' interests and in increasing minority representation (Chandler and Grofman 1994). Prior to the passage of the VRA, minority legislators had a hard time getting elected, in part, because laws were passed to prevent minorities from participating in politics.

The VRA's passage led to a dramatic increase in the number of blacks who registered and voted. The effect was particularly profound in the Deep South (Black and Black 1987). In Mississippi, the percentage of African Americans qualified to vote went from less than 7 percent in 1964 to nearly 60 percent in 1968 (Thurber 2004, 543; Wasniewski 2008). These improvements led to a marked increase in the number of African American elected officials. The number of African American members in the U.S. House in 1971 was more than double the number who had served in 1965. The changes at the state level were equally apparent. In 1965 there were only seventy-two black elected officials in the eleven states that were part of the original Confederacy. Just a decade later, more than fifteen hundred black officials held office (Wasniewski 2008, 272).

A key component of the VRA, and one reason for its success, is that it required states that had a history of discrimination to obtain preclearance before they could make any changes that affected voting procedures. In the years prior to the VRA, poll taxes, all-white primaries, literacy tests, and so on had been used to prevent black participation. The preclearance requirement prevented these laws from being implemented in the first place. This aspect of the VRA and its focus on states with a history of discrimination have also been at the heart of controversies about law. In 2006, for example, when the renewal of the VRA was being debated, some officials from southern states argued that their states should no longer be subject to the provision because the levels of racism had diminished and the cost of preclearance was high (Hernandez 2006; Kellman 2006).

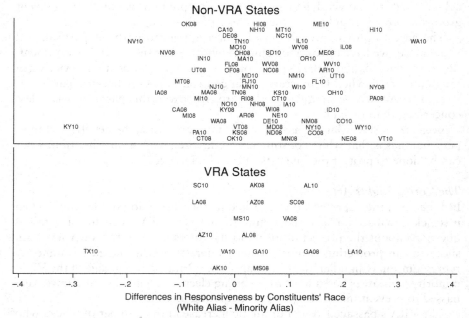

FIGURE 6.2. State-by-state results on the treatment of whites relative to minorities. This figure displays the level of bias among white state legislators for each state in the 2008 and 2010 studies (minority legislators are dropped when calculating values). The bias is measured by taking the difference, across the state, between how many responded to the white alias(es) and how many responded to the minority alias(es) used in the study. The top panel shows the distribution of results for the states not subject to the preclearance requirement of the VRA and the bottom panel the distribution of results for the states subject to the preclearance requirement. The *y*-axis is not informative, and the observations only take different values on this axis to improve the presentation.

In June 2013 the Supreme Court weighed in on this issue (*Shelby County, Alabama v. Holder*) and struck down section 4 of the VRA, which effectively ended the power of the preclearance requirement. In the majority opinion of a 5–4 vote, Chief Justice Roberts wrote, "Our country has changed and while any racial discrimination in voting is too much, Congress must ensure that the legislation it passes to remedy that problem speaks to current conditions." In reaching this conclusion, the court made two major points. First, it did not think the latest available data showed evidence of racial bias in the states requiring preclearance. Second, the burden of preclearance was not a burden that all states shared equally.

In light of these conclusions, Figure 6.2 presents the level of bias among state legislators for each state in the 2008 and 2010 studies. Each observation represents the percentage of state legislators who responded to the white alias minus the percentage of legislators who responded to the minority alias in that state. Positive values thus indicate that the state legislators were more responsive to the putative white constituents than the putative minority constituents. For this calculation I limit the sample to the white state legislators. The top panel shows the distribution of results for states not subject to the preclearance requirement of the VRA and the bottom panel for states subject to the preclearance requirement.

As Figure 6.2 shows, the legislators in the majority of states subject to the VRA preclearance requirement exhibit bias in favor of white constituents (about two-thirds of these states exhibit a positive bias in favor of white constituents). In this regard, the court was wrong in concluding that bias is no longer a problem in these states. Legislators in the states subject to preclearance exhibit a personal bias in favor of white constituents. However, the court was correct that these states are not outliers. The top half of Figure 6.2 shows that the majority of legislators in other states exhibit the same racial bias. In other words, state legislators – the individuals who are responsible for passing state election laws – exhibit personal racial bias.

Of course one caveat is that these results only reveal legislators' personal biases. These results do not necessarily indicate what laws the legislators would pass. It is entirely possible that even though legislators in the Northeast exhibit the same levels of personal bias, they would not pass laws that are racially discriminatory because of the state culture. Or perhaps southern legislators would do better because past experience with discrimination makes them more senstive to the issue. Either way, the results provide support for the notion that racial discrimination exists in politics and suggest that removing protections against discrimination are likely to hurt minorities' interests.

The Role of Racial Redistricting
Racial redistricting, another practice that emerged from debates about the VRA, aims to create districts where minorities are a large enough voting bloc to enable them to elect a candidate of their choice. Typically a candidate who is of the same race or ethnicity as these voters represents such districts. However, in creating minority districts, there are fewer minorities, and hence fewer Democrats, in the surrounding districts. Thus, although the use of majority-minority districts increases the number of minority candidates elected, it also decreases the number of Democrats in office because Democratic voters are concentrated in a relatively small number of districts (Lublin 1997; see also Overby and Cosgrove 1996). A point of contention is whether minorities' interests are better served by majority-minority districts.

Swain (1993) argues that majority-minority districts make minorities worse off because partisanship, not race, is a key determinant of how well politicians represent minority constituents' interests. In other words, Swain argues that white Democrats do an equally good job representing minority constituents.

The results here challenge that claim. White Democrats are not a good substitute for minority Democrats. White Democrats exhibit the same level and type of bias that white Republicans do. Majority-minority districts serve an important role in protecting the interests of minority voters and ensuring that their voice is heard in the legislative process (see also, among others, Canon 1999; Wallace 2010; Minta 2011).

7

Bias in Politics

As a discipline, political science's dominant paradigm for understanding elections and representation is rooted in analogies between elections and economic transactions. Rather than trading goods and services, citizens give their votes to politicians who offer their preferred policy positions (e.g., Downs 1957; Adams, Merrill, and Grofman 2005).

Using the economics paradigm, most research on inequality and representation has primarily looked to differences in levels of participation as the source of this bias (Verba 2003; APSA Task Force 2004). The argument is that politicians favor some groups because those voters are more likely to vote or are more likely to support the candidate if the candidate helps them (Bartels 1998). The implication is that if groups participated at equal levels, they would enjoy equal levels of representation.

Though common, the view that equal participation would secure equal treatment is wrong. In Chapter 4, for example, I showed that when a janitor and an attorney write the same letter, using the same arguments, politicians systematically discount the janitor's views. Similarly, in Chapter 6 I showed that when minorities and whites write letters to legislators asking for help, legislators systematically give better service to the constituents from their same racial group. The advantage of these experiments is that the e-mails sent to legislators are simple and held constant; the constituents are making the same requests. The favored groups in these cases do not have better connections or better arguments; they are favored simply because they are part of the right group.[1]

---

[1] I do not want to dismiss the importance of voters' political participation. The experiments in Chapter 6 show that politicians are sensitive to signals about a constituent's partisanship and likely level of participation. Legislators were, for example, significantly more likely to help constituents who signaled that they were copartisans with their request about learning how to register to vote. Still, these differences were actually smaller in size than the levels of bias related to race.

Politicians' Background as a Source of Inequality

If voters' level of political activity does not explain why they are unequally represented (see Bartels 2008), what does? I have argued, and found evidence, that politicians, and more specifically their backgrounds, are an important source of political inequality.

Politicians come to office with information, attitudes, and biases that lead to inequality in representation. In other words, bias cannot be wholly explained by differences in constituents' input; instead the characteristics of the politicians providing the outputs are an important source of bias. I have outlined two ways in which politicians' background leads to bias.

First, politicians are not neutral parties. The results in Chapters 4 and 6 show that politicians exhibit favoritism toward some constituents over others. The experiments in Chapter 6, for example, show that politicians are less responsive to constituents who are not from their racial group. This bias occurs even though the putative constituents are making the same requests. Further, this racial bias cannot be explained by strategic considerations to favor copartisans or likely voters. Instead, legislators of all races and parties exhibit a marked favoritism toward constituents from their in-group. Politicians come to office with personal preferences, and these preferences lead to bias in representation.

Second, politicians come to office with different information, knowledge, and sets of experiences that make it easier for them to work on issues important to people like them. These differences lead to bias because they incentivize politicians to focus on the issue(s) that are most important to people like them. Rational politicians focus on these issues because it allows them to maximize the output they care about – reelection – while expending the least amount of resources (Downs 1957, 5). Politicians are simply playing to their strengths.

The experiments in Chapter 5 confirm this argument by showing that politicians' personal knowledge allows them to more easily help those most like them. This is exactly the behavior we expect from rational officials: they should work on the issues for which their personal knowledge makes it is less costly to do so.

How Differences in Information Lead to Bias in the Aggregate

One of the great sources of inequality, as a result of politicians' rational behavior of focusing on issues they know a lot about, is that some constituents are numerically better represented in office. Melancton Smith foresaw this issue during the debate over the U.S. Constitution. During New York's ratifying convention in 1788, Smith argued:

The idea that naturally suggests itself to our minds, when we speak of representatives is, that they resemble those they represent; they should be a true picture of the people; possess the knowledge of their circumstances and their wants; sympathize in all their distresses, and be disposed to seek their true interests. The knowledge necessary for the representatives of a free people, not only comprehends extensive political and commercial information, such as is acquired by men of refined education, who have leisure to attain to high degrees of improvement, but it should also comprehend that kind of acquaintance with the common concerns and occupations of the people, which men of the middling class of life are in general much better competent to, than those of a superior class. (Quoted in Storing 1981, 6.12.9)

One of the significant factors in American government is the overwhelming degree to which government service is the sole province of the wealthy (Carnes 2012). The majority of officials across all three branches of the federal government are millionaires. Because millionaires will have more personal experience with estate planning than navigating the welfare system, the former issue will receive undue attention while the latter suffers from inattention.

Of course it is not only the agenda that will be biased. Differences in information can also affect the quality of the policy decisions that are reached. Politicians do not always have information about the likely policy consequences of different options. They often rely on the information provided by other public officials (Krehbiel 1991). If groups are numerically underrepresented in office, there will be a smaller pool of quality information providers that can be drawn on when making policy.

Significantly, the bias that arises because of legislators' information deficit is not driven by overt bias. Instead, politicians' rational decisions to focus on the things they know best lead to political inequality for numerically underrepresented groups because the issues those groups care about naturally get less attention.

Will These Biases Go Away?

In assessing the prospects of continuing bias in representation it is worth separately considering two sources: bias driven by personal attitudes and preferences and bias driven by a legislator's information deficit and rational electoral interests. With regard to the bias driven by a politician's personal attitudes, some theoretical models suggest that this bias will naturally end without intervention. The dominant model of elections and politics, for example, borrows insights from economics, where, at least theoretically, the profit motive should eradicate discrimination. If some businesses discriminate against certain types of workers, other employers should be able to offer products of the same quality at lower prices by hiring the workers who are discriminated against. This should cause businesses that discriminate to become less profitable and eventually go out of business.

In politics, representatives engaging in discrimination do not face the same threat because they only need a plurality of votes to retain their offices. Elected policymakers can easily obtain a plurality of votes while discriminating against a minority group of voters in their districts. A challenger can attract those voters who are discriminated against by treating them equally. However, because these voters are a minority in the district, winning them over is insufficient to unseat an incumbent. Minority voters are not swing voters and therefore are likely to be ignored (Frymer 1999). Consequently, there are few reasons to expect arbitrage to operate in the representation relationship between voters and policymakers. Indeed, theories about the political market expect representatives to focus on some voters to the detriment of others (Fenno 1978; Bartels 1998). Because discrimination continues to occur in the economic marketplace (Arrow 1998), even though there are good theoretical reasons to expect it to be eradicated, it is unlikely that personal biases will cease to affect politics (where there are theoretical reasons to expect bias).

In contrast, there may be things that could be done to affect the level of bias driven by legislators' electoral interests. In particular, the results in Chapter 5 suggest that bias arises in part because legislators efficiently seek their goal of winning reelection. This drive for reelection leads legislators to focus on the issues they know most about. This source of bias may be affected by changing aspects of access to office. As politicians who have information about the issues that matter to underrepresented groups gain more access to public office, the information deficit responsible for this bias will be ameliorated. The creation of majority-minority districts is one example of a successful program aimed at increasing access to office for racial minorities (I discuss racial redistricting more in what follows).

In other areas, however, access to office is decreasing. Politicians from working-class backgrounds have always been one of the most underrepresented groups in office, and yet in recent decades this discrepancy has widened (Carnes 2012). There are many potential culprits behind this pattern, but the increasing cost of running a campaign is likely a contributing factor. In this regard, recent developments do not offer much hope. In the wake of the Supreme Court's *Citizens United* (2010) decision, the cost of running a campaign is only likely to increase and lead to greater levels of economic inequality in terms of who serves.

Different Groups, Different Biases

Because politics is unlikely to self-correct for the existing biases, we need to understand those biases in order to develop institutions that ameliorate them. One of the important implications of this book is that not all groups face the same biases.

This is an important contribution because studies finding statistically significant levels of discrimination are more likely to be published (Gerber, Green, and Nickerson 2001; Gerber and Malhotra 2008). Studies finding discrimination are more likely to be published both because researchers are more likely to stop working on papers with statistically insignificant findings (Mahoney 1977)

TABLE 7.1. *When Does Representation Break Down? Experimental Results by Subpopulation*

		Evaluating Constituent Opinion	Informational Inequalities	Output Stage
Demographic Group	Gender	No	Yes	No
	Race/Ethnicity	No	Not Tested	Yes
	SES	Yes	Yes	No

Notes: This table summarizes the results of the experiments found in Chapters 4–6. "Yes" indicates that the experiment found evidence of bias for that demographic group at that stage. "No" indicates that the experiment did not yield evidence of bias against that demographic group.

and because editors and referees are more likely to reject papers that show statistically insignificant effects (Iyengar and Greenhouse 1988). As a result of these reporting practices, we do not see the cases in which discrimination is not a problem.

One of the advantages of my research is that I look at bias in representation for different groups in different parts of the process. By studying and *reporting* the results of various studies of the process, we can see more clearly where we are failing and need to make improvements. Knowing both the failures and the successes allows us to more effectively allocate our resources to correct for inequalities in representation.

Table 7.1 summarizes the findings of my experiments about when different groups face discrimination. One striking finding is the lack of gender discrimination. Public officials do not engage in gender discrimination at either the input or the output stages of the representation process.

While I do not find any gender bias at the input or output stages, public officials do exhibit bias at both. They exhibit bias against racial minorities at the output stage, but not at the input stage. This pattern is reversed for low-SES individuals. Public officials exhibit bias against low-SES constituents at the input stage, but not at the output stage.

Discounting the Opinions of Low-SES Constituents

The discounting of low-SES constituents' opinions serves to highlight the concerns raised by recent studies showing the weak correlation between policy outcomes and the preferences of low-income constituents (Bartels 2008; Gilens 2012). The researchers conducting these studies have raised the concern that public officials are ignoring low-income voters' interests.

However, the positive correlation between high-income constituents' preferences and policy outcomes need not necessarily mean that public officials are biased against low-income constituents. The positive correlation could arise if legislators are acting as trustees and the legislators and high-income constituents are more informed than low-income constituents. In that case, what appears to be bias would arise naturally from differences in knowledge. This explanation also has very different normative implications. The idea that legislators are less responsive to low-income constituents' preferences raises concerns that they are worse off. However, if instead legislators are acting as trustees and doing what they think is best for their constituents even when it is contrary to their constituents' opinions, then there will be bias in the representation of the constituents' *preferences* but not necessarily their *interests*. In fact, low-income constituents may actually have better outcomes if legislators act as trustees as opposed to delegates.

The strength of the research design in Chapter 4 is that the e-mail that public officials evaluated was simple and the contents were held constant. Both the janitor and the attorney expressed the same positions using the same arguments. Because the only difference was the profession of the writer, we can attribute the difference in the elected officials' behavior to the writer's profession. When constituents put forth similar arguments and exhibit similar levels of engagement, public officials give more credence to the opinions of high-income individuals. This bias is not the result of legislators trying to better serve constituents' interests.

Why Is There Less Discrimination along Gender Lines?

One recent study examined whether men's or women's preferences better predicted legislators' roll call votes and found that both groups' preferences are equally represented (Griffin, Newman, and Wolbrecht 2012). My results are consistent with gender equality in politics. Legislators do not engage in gender discrimination at either the input or the output stage even though they exhibit bias at these stages against other groups. Why is there less gender discrimination than race and economic discrimination?

One likely possibility is that our social networks are strongly divided along racial and economic lines. Most Americans live in neighborhoods that are divided by race and income. We also often spend our free social time interacting with people from our own racial groups and income classes (McPherson, Smith-Lovin, and Cook 2001). By contrast we do not live in gender-segregated neighborhoods, and our social networks are much less likely to be divided by gender. This is all reinforced by the very structure of the family. Within households we have gender diversity. Because we have meaningful interactions with individuals of the opposite gender we are less likely to hold biases against them. Similar patterns of interaction explain why some groups – those that are less likely to interact meaningfully with their neighbors – face greater levels of religious discrimination (Putnam and Campbell 2010).

While I do not find any direct discrimination along gender lines, I do find that women have more information about women's issues than men and so are more likely to work on those issues. The underrepresentation of women, therefore, may result in less attention to women's issues. Thus, if bias occurs we should expect it to appear in the agenda and/or quality of legislation related to gender issues, not in the way legislators vote on that agenda. My experiments were not designed to test for bias in the agenda and quality of legislation by issue area, but the results point to the legislative agenda as a focal area for further study by practitioners and academics studying gender equality in politics.

Potential Solutions for Improving Representation

Understanding the bias that different groups face can help us design institutions to improve representation. In what follows I discuss a few modest possibilities along these lines.

Multimember Districts as a Way to Improve Overall Levels of Representation

In Chapter 5, I found evidence that descriptive representation provides an informational advantage. Female officials are more likely to have personal knowledge about issues that are important to female constituents. Similarly, officials from low-income areas are more likely to be able to answer questions of interest to low-income constituents.

A key feature of this informational advantage is that the benefits need not come at a cost to other constituents. The term *Pareto improvement* is used to describe the situation that occurs when the benefits for the group that is being represented do not come at a cost to others. An informational advantage is often Pareto improving, as the information that legislators bring to office can improve the quality of deliberation and lead to better policy outcomes for everyone (Gilligan and Krehbiel 1989, 1990; Krehbiel 1991; Mansbridge 1999).

A major benefit of multimember districts is that each legislator comes to office with unique experiences and information on different topics. Legislators in multimember districts can use that knowledge to specialize in different issues that are important in the district and provide Pareto-improving representation. This dynamic helps explain Wendy Schiller's conclusion about representation in the U.S. Senate.

If we incorporate the two-person nature of Senate delegations and the multidimensionality of legislative behavior into our evaluation of Senate representation, we can conclude that representation in the U.S. Senate is better than it is commonly believed to be. When two senators from the same state are viewed as a pair, it is clear that their combined representational agendas include a wide range of interests and opinions that exists among constituents in their state. (2000, 165)

Snyder and Ueda (2007) have shown that cities represented by multimember districts also secure more funding from the legislature than those that are represented by the same number of legislators in single-member districts.

Further, the results in Chapter 3 highlight the benefit of having multimember districts with staggered elections. The 2009 and 2010 experiments (see Table 3.1) showed that legislators become less responsive when they decide to retire. This is consistent with earlier results showing that legislators provide less representation to their constituents after they decide to retire (Rothenberg and Sanders 2000). In multimember districts with staggered elections, it is very rare for both legislators to retire at the same time. Consequently, constituents in multimember districts have at least one representative who is always actively considering their interests. There may be other costs to multimember districts that have not been tested, but the results here, combined with the findings in the literature, suggest that multimember districts give constituents better overall levels of representation.

Which Districts Maximize the Political Interests of Minority Voters?

Racial redistricting is another area in which electoral institutions related to districting can affect representation. Racial redistricting aims to promote these interests by creating districts in which minorities can elect a candidate of their choice (Hajnal 2009). The surest way to accomplish this goal is to create majority-minority districts in which the minority group represents at least 50 percent of the voters. Significantly, legislators elected from such districts are typically members of the minority group. Another approach is to create what Christian Grose (2011) labels minority decisive districts. These are districts in which the minority group is a decisive part – say, 40 percent of the voters in the district – of a coalition with white voters such that they would likely elect a candidate of color. A third option is to create influence districts in which, although the minority group does not represent a numerical majority or even a decisive part of the coalition, it is large enough to control an election's outcome when its members vote as a bloc (e.g., when the support of nonminority voters for the two candidates is fairly evenly split). These districts are likely to elect a white candidate who shares the partisan affiliation of the minority voters, which in most cases means the candidate will be a Democrat. A fourth approach is not to engage in racial redistricting at all. Some argue that racial redistricting hurts minority interests because it concentrates the minority's power in a relative small number of districts at the cost of their influence in other districts. These critics raise concerns that the approach results in the election of more Republicans, who are more likely to pursue policies contrary minority voters' interests.

The four options represent a continuum of the extent to which minority voters are concentrated in one district versus spread out across several districts. The more voters are concentrated, the more likely they are to be represented by someone from their minority group and the more likely it is that voters, both minorities and whites, will be represented by a descriptive legislator. The trade-off, as already noted, is that these minority voters' influence in other districts becomes increasingly diminished the more they are concentrated in a small number of districts. Determining which of the four approaches maximizes the political interests of minority voters overall – that is, determining the point on the continuum that maximizes their interests – first requires knowing whether descriptive representation leads to better substantive representation.

Swain (1993) has argued that white Democrats provide black voters the same level of substantive representation as black Democrats do. Her argument suggests that the party of the legislator is much more important than his or her race. Lublin (1997) concurs with this position; he found that black and white legislators vote differently, but that these racial differences are small relative to the differences between Democrats and Republicans. These researchers thus argue that white Democrats are a good substitute for minority Democrats.

If white Democrats are in fact a good substitute for minority Democrats, then concentrating minority voters into relatively small numbers of districts is a net negative. While it results in the election of more minority Democrats, it comes at the cost of an even greater number of white Democrats losing seats. Put another way, if descriptive representation does not lead to substantive benefits, then racial redistricting, if done at all, should focus only on creating influence districts.

My results show, however, that this conclusion – at least as it relates to constituency service – is based on a faulty assumption. Legislators' race and ethnicity predict how they treat constituents, but their partisanship does not. White Democrats and white Republicans exhibited similar levels of in-group personal bias; thus, white Democrats are not a good substitute for minority Democrats. If racial redistricting is to extend the interests of minority voters, then it should focus on approaches that elect more minority representatives.

Both majority-minority and minority-decisive districts should elect minority legislators. Which of these two approaches maximizes voters' political interests? To answer that question we need to understand where the benefits of descriptive representation are likely to be felt.

Most research on descriptive representation has focused on legislators' roll call votes (e.g., Lublin 1997; Hood and Morris 1998; Hutchings 1998; Swers 1998; Tate 2003; Carnes 2012). However, Christian Grose (2011) shows that the benefits are unlikely to be felt at the policy level because elected minority officials would not be a large enough coalition to influence roll call outcomes. Instead, the benefit is likely to be felt at the level of the individual constituent. My experiments have shown that elected officials exhibit in-group, personal discrimination by race/ethnicity, but not gender or SES, in their direct interactions with individual constituents. Legislators receive thousands of e-mails and letters each year asking for help (Fitch and Goldsmidt 2005), and both white and minority officials are likely to be biased toward helping constituents from their own racial and ethnic groups. Thus, more preference should be given to

districting schemes that maximize the likelihood of descriptive representation
by race and ethnicity – that is, creating majority-minority districts (cf. Grose
2011).

Diverse Staffs: Another Way to Improve Representation for All Groups

Although governments can implement various electoral reforms to improve
the representation of underrepresented groups, these policies often involve
tradeoffs that make these policies controversial and therefore difficult to realize.
A less controversial step is for public officials to increase the diversity of their
staffs.

Elected officials increasingly rely on staff. Salisbury and Shepsle (1981a,b)
argue that staff members do so much of the legislative work that it makes
sense to consider the legislative enterprise as a whole, which includes those
staff members, as the relevant actor in the representation relationship. There
are tradeoffs associated with relying more on staff members, but there are
also benefits. One is that legislators benefit from the personal knowledge and
experience that staff members bring with them. Chapter 5 shows that legislators use their own personal experience to better represent their constituents.
Ultimately, however, any given elected official is but one person with one set
of experiences from which to draw. When elected officials assemble diverse
staffs for their offices, those offices benefit from the knowledge and experience
that each member brings. This diverse knowledge can be used to help inform
both constituency service and policy as elected officials strive to use the best
information available to represent their constituents.

The experiments in Chapter 5 show how public officials already rely to some
extent on the knowledge and experience of their staffs. In the study of state
legislators, one legislative assistant prefaced the answer to the question in our
e-mail by writing that "Rep. [redacted] asked me to check into this for you since
I've had similar experiences, and I found. . . ." In response to a question about
an advanced placement program question, one mayor responded as follows.

I checked with our Administrative Assistant, [redacted], whose son is graduating from
[redacted] High this year. She spoke very highly of the school, said they have an advanced
placement program, an honors program and a dual enrollment program for Seniors with
[redacted] College.

The best evidence suggests, however, that officials may not always assemble
diverse staffs. Grose, Mangum, and Martin (2007; see also Grose 2011) find
that white legislators are more likely to hire white staffs and black legislators
black staffs, even when controlling for the composition of the district. If legislators want to maximize the benefits to constituents and themselves of relying on
staff members more, they should seek out diverse assistants who can provide
information and knowledge drawn from their personal experiences.

Concluding Thoughts

Researchers studying representation and inequality should continue to pay attention to the role of unequal participation. Although my findings show that participation cannot fully explain the existing inequality, these findings all relate to politicians elected under the current equilibrium in which some underrepresented constituents are less likely to participate. It may be the case that if there were sustained equality in participation then the politicians elected under those alternative conditions might be more evenhanded.

This optimistic prediction must be tempered by the reality that inequality is driven in part by the fact that politicians want to be reelected. The desire to win office and its associated incentives will always be with us. Because politicians are playing to their strengths by focusing on the issues they know best, there will always be incentives that lead to bias. Even if politicians' personal biases no longer played a role, these strategic incentives would remain.

Bias will remain unless there is equality in *elite political participation*. Because bias is driven by who comes to office, equality in mass participation would likely diminish political inequality but would not eliminate it. While we should continue to study the role of mass participation in affecting inequality and representation, we must also do more to understand elite political participation.

The need to study candidate emergence reflects the reality that we cannot look to participation as a panacea for bias in the current system. The results here show that even when constituents participate at equal rates, politicians exhibit significant levels of bias against some of them. The root of this bias begins before politicians even come to office. *Politicians are not exchangeable;* they enter office with attitudes, preferences, and information that shape how they act and who they favor. Understanding inequalities in representation requires understanding what determines who serves. We need to understand more about what determines who runs for office.

References

Adams, James F., Samuel Merrill, III, and Bernard Grofman. 2005. *A Unified Theory of Party Competition*. New York: Cambridge University Press.

Adida, Claire L., David D. Laitin, and Marie-Ann Valfort. 2010. "Identifying Barriers to Muslim Integration in France." *Proceedings of the National Academy of Sciences* 107 (52): 22384–22390.

Adler, E. Scott, and John S. Lapinski. 1997. "Demand-Side Theory and Congressional Committee Composition: A Constituency Characteristics Approach." *American Journal of Political Science* 41 (3): 895–918.

Angrist, Joshua D., and Jorn-Steffen Pischke. 2009. *Mostly Harmless Econometrics: An Empiricist's Companion*. Princeton, NJ: Princeton University Press.

Ansolabehere, Stephen. 2009. Cooperative Congressional Election Study, 2008: Common Content [Computer File]. Release 1: February 2, 2009. Cambridge, MA: M.I.T.

APSA Task Force. 2004. "American Democracy in an Age of Rising Inequality." *Perspectives on Politics* 2 (4): 651–666.

Arnold, R. Douglas, and Nicholas Carnes. 2012. "Holding Mayors Accountable: New York's Executives from Koch to Bloomberg." *American Journal of Political Science* 56 (4): 949–963.

Arrow, Kenneth J. 1998. "What Has Economics to Say about Racial Discrimination?" *Journal of Economic Perspectives* 12 (2): 91–100.

Barone, Michael, and Grant Ujifusa. 1995. *The Almanac of American Politics 1994*. Washington, DC: National Journal.

Barreto, Matt. 2007. "¡Si Se Puede! Latino Candidates and the Mobilization of Latino Voters." *American Political Science Review* 101 (3): 425–441.

———. 2010. *Ethnic Cues: The Role of Shared Ethnicity in Latino Political Participation*. University of Michigan Press.

Bartels, Larry M. 1998. "Where the Ducks Are: Voting Power in a Party System." In *Politicians and Party Politics*, ed. John G. Geer. Baltimore, MD: Johns Hopkins University Press, 43–79.

———. 2008. *Unequal Democracy: The Political Economy of the New Gilded Age.* New York: Russell Sage.

Beckwith, Karen. 2007. "Numbers and Newness: The Descriptive and Substantive Representation of Women." *Canadian Journal of Political Science* 40 (1): 27–49.

Bergan, Daniel E. 2009. "Does Grassroots Lobbying Work? A Field Experiment Measuring the Effects of an e-Mail Lobbying Campaign on Legislative Behavior." *American Politics Research* 37 (2): 327–352.

Berkman, Michael B., and Robert E. O'Connor. 1993. "Do Women Legislators Matter? Female Legislators and State Abortion Policy." *American Politics Research* 21 (1): 102–124.

Bertrand, Marianne, and Sendhil Mullainathan. 2004. "Are Emily and Greg More Employable than Lakisha and Jamal? A Field Experiment on Labor Market Discrimination." *American Economic Review* 94 (4): 991–1013.

Bianco, William T. 1994. *Trust: Representatives and Constituents.* Ann Arbor, MI: University of Michigan Press.

Black, Earl, and Merle Black. 1987. *Politics and Society in the South.* Cambridge, MA: Harvard University Press.

Blumenthal, Sidney. 1980. *The Permanent Campaign: Inside the World of Elite Political Operations.* Boston: Beacon Press.

Bobo, Lawrence. 2001. "Racial Attitudes and Relations at the Close of the Twentieth Century." In *America Becoming: Racial Trends and Their Consequences*, vol. 1, ed. Neil J. Smelser, William J. Wilson, and Faith Mitchell. Washington, DC: National Academy Press, 264–301.

Bobo, Lawrence, and Camille L. Zubrinsky. 1996. "Attitudes on Residential Integration: Perceived Status Differences, Mere In-Group Preference, or Racial Prejudice?" *Social Forces* 74 (3): 883–909.

Bratton, Kathleen A. 2005. "Critical Mass Theory Revisited: The Behavior and Success of Token Women in State Legislatures." *Politics and Gender* 1 (1): 97–125.

Bratton, Kathleen A., and Kerry L. Haynie. 1999. "Agenda Setting and Legislative Success in State Legislatures: The Effect of Gender and Race." *Journal of Politics* 61 (3): 658–679.

Broockman, David E. 2013. "Black Politicians Are More Intrinsically Motivated to Advance Blacks' Interests: A Field Experiment Manipulating Political Incentives." *American Journal of Political Science* 57 (3): 521–536.

Burden, Barry C. 2007. *Personal Roots of Representation.* Princeton, NJ: Princeton University Press.

Burrell, Barbara C. 1994. *A Woman's Place in the House: Campaigning for Congress in the Feminist Era.* Ann Arbor, MI: University of Michigan Press.

Butler, Daniel M. 2013. "Why Are Politicians Sometimes Unresponsive to Public Opinion? Experimental Evidence of How Public Officials Justify Discounting Constituents' Opinions They Disagree With." Prepared for the 2013 *State Politics and Policy Conference*, Iowa City, Iowa, May 23–25, 2013.

Butler, Daniel M., and David E. Broockman. 2011. "Do Politicians Racially Discriminate against Constituents? A Field Experiment on State Legislators." *American Journal of Political Science* 55 (3): 463–477.

Butler, Daniel M., and Matthew J. Butler. 2006. "Splitting the Difference? Causal Inference and Theories of Split-party Delegations." *Political Analysis* 14 (4): 439–455.

Butler, Daniel M., and Thad Kousser. 2013. "How do Public Goods Providers Play Public Goods Games?" Paper prepared for the *13th Annual State Politics and Policy Conference*, Iowa City, Iowa, May 23–25, 2013.

Butler, Daniel M., and David W. Nickerson. 2011. "Can Learning Constituency Opinion Affect how Legislators Vote? Results from a Field Experiment." *Quarterly Journal of Political Science* 6 (1): 55–83.

Butler, Daniel M., and Eleanor Neff Powell. 2014. "Understanding the Party Brand: Experimental Evidence on the Role of Valence." *Journal of Politics* 76 (2): 492–505.

Butler, Daniel M., Christopher Karpowitz, and Jeremy C. Pope. 2011. "Who Gets the Credit? Legislative Responsiveness and Evaluations of Members, Parties, and the US Congress." Working Manuscript. Yale University.

———. 2012. "A Field Experiment on Legislators' Home Style: Service versus Policy." *Journal of Politics* 74 (2): 474–486.

Cain, Bruce E., John Ferejohn, and Morris P. Fiorina. 1987. *The Personal Vote: Constituency Service and Electoral Independence*. Cambridge: Harvard University Press.

Callander, Steven. 2008. "A Theory of Policy Expertise." *Quarterly Journal of Political Science* 3 (2): 123–140.

Cameron, Charles, David Epstein, and Sharyn O'Halloran. 1996. "Do Majority-Minority Districts Maximize Substantive Black Representation in Congress?" *American Political Science Review* 90 (4): 794–812.

Canon, David T. 1999. *Race, Redistricting, and Representation: The Unintended Consequences of Black Majority Districts*. Chicago: University of Chicago Press.

Carnes, Nicholas. 2012. "Does the Numerical Underrepresentation of the Working Class in Congress Matter? Evidence from Roll Call Voting in the House of Representatives." *Legislative Studies Quarterly* 37 (1): 5–34.

Census of Governments, U.S. Census Bureau. 2007. Current Spending of Public Elementary-Secondary School Systems by State, State and Local Government Finances by Level of Government and State, and Public School System Finances for Elementary-Secondary Education by State.

Center for American Women and Politics (CAWP). 2011. "Women in State Legislatures 2011."

Chandler, Davidson, and Bernard Grofman, eds. 1994. *Quiet Revolution in the South: The Impact of the Voting Rights Act, 1965–1990*. Princeton, NJ: Princeton University Press.

Chattopadhyay, Raghabendra, and Esther Duflo. 2004. "Women as Policy Makers: Evidence from a Randomized Policy Experiment in India." *Econometrica* 72 (5): 1409–1443.

Considine, Mark, and Iva Ellen Deutchman. 1994. "The Gendering of Political Institutions: A Comparison of American and Australian State Legislators." *Social Science Quarterly* 75 (4): 854–866.

Converse, Philip E. 1964. "The Nature of Belief Systems in Mass Publics." In *Ideology and Discontent* ed., David Apter, pages 206–261.

Cover, Albert D. and Bruce S. Brumberg. 1982. "Baby Books and Ballots: The Impact of Congressional Mail on Constituent Opinion." *The American Political Science Review* 76 (2): 347–359.

Cyert, Richard M., and James G. March. 1963. *A Behavioral Theory of the Firm*. Englewood Cliffs, NJ: Prentice-Hall.

Dahl, Robert A. 1967. *Pluralist Democracy in the United States: Conflict and Consent.* Chicago: Rand McNally.

Darcy, Robert. 1996. "Women in the State Legislative Power Structure: Committee Chairs." *Social Science Quarterly* 77 (4): 888–898.

Dawson, Michael C. 1994. *Behind the Mule: Race and Class in African-American Politics.* Princeton, NJ: Princeton University Press.

Dexter, Lewis A. 1964. "The Good Will of the Important People: More on the Jeopardy of the Interview." *Public Opinion Quarterly* 28 (4): 556–563.

Diamond, Irene. 1977. *Sex Roles in the State House.* New Haven, CT: Yale University Press.

Dodson, Debra L. 1998. "Representing Women's Interests in the U.S. House of Representatives." In *Women and Elective Office: Past, Present, and Future.* eds. Sue Thomas and Clyde Wilcox. New York: Oxford University Press.

———. 2006. *The Impact of Women in Congress.* New York: Oxford University Press.

Dodson, Debra L., and Susan Carroll. 1991. *Reshaping the Agenda: Women in State Legislatures.* New Brunswick: Center for American Women and Politics, Rutgers, The State University of New Jersey.

Dolan, Julie. 1997. "Support for Women's Interests in the 103rd Congress: The Distinct Impact of Congressional Women." *Women & Politics* 18 (4): 81–94.Dolan, Kathleen. 2006. "Symbolic Mobilization? The Impact of Candidate Sex in American Elections." *American Politics Research* 34 (6): 687–704.

Dolan, Kathleen, and Lynn Ford. 1995. "Women in the State Legislatures: Feminist Identity and Legislative Behavior." *American Politics Quarterly* 23 (1): 96–108.

Downs, Anthony. 1957. *An Economic Theory of Democracy.* New York: Harper Collins.

Druckman, James and Lawrence Jacobs. 2011. "Segmented Representation: The Reagan White House and Disproportionate Responsiveness." In *Who Gets Represented?*, ed. Peter Enns and Christopher Wlezien. New York: Russell Sage.

Ellis, Christopher. 2012. "Understanding Economic Biases in Representation: Income, Resources, and Policy Representation in the 110th House." *Political Research Quarterly* 65 (4): 938–951.

Erikson, Robert and Yosef Bhatti. 2011. "How Poorly are the Poor Represented in the US Senate?" In *Who Gets Represented?* Peter Enns and Christopher Wlezien, eds. pp. 223–246. New York: Russell Sage.

Esteban, Joan, and Debraj Ray. 2006. "Inequality, Lobbying, and Resource Allocation." *American Economic Review* 96 (1): 257–279.

Eulau, Heinz, and Paul D. Karps. 1977. "The Puzzle of Representation: Specifying Components of Responsiveness." *Legislative Studies Quarterly* 2 (3): 233–254.

Fenno, Richard F. 1973. *Congressmen in Committees.* Boston: Little, Brown.

———. 1978. *Home Style: House Members in their Districts.* Boston: Little, Brown and Company.

Fiorina, Morris P. 1981. *Retrospective Voting in American Elections.* New Haven, CT: Yale University Press.

———. 1989. *Congress: Keystone of the Washington Establishment*, 2nd ed. New Haven, CT: Yale University Press.

Fisher, Samuel H., III, and Rebekah Herrick. 2013. "Old versus New: The Comparative Efficiency of Mail and Internet Surveys of State Legislators." *State Politics & Policy Quarterly* 13(2): 147–163.

Fitch, Brad, and Kathy Goldschmidt. 2005. *Communicating with Congress: How Capitol Hill is Coping with the Surge in Citizen Advocacy*. Washington, DC: Congressional Management Foundation.

Fix, Michael and Margery A. Turner, eds. 1998. *A National Report Card on Discrimination in America: The Role of Testing*. Washington, DC: Urban Institute Press.

Foerstel, Karen, and Herbert Foerstel. 1996. *Climbing the Hill: Gender Conflict in Congress*. Westport, CT: Praeger Publishers.

Fryer, Roland G., Jr., and Steven D. Levitt. 2004. "The Causes and Consequences of Distinctively Black Names." *Quarterly Journal of Economics* 119 (3): 767–805.

Frymer, Paul. 1999. *Uneasy Alliances: Race and Party Competition in America*. Princeton, NJ: Princeton University Press.

Gabel, Matthew, and Kenneth Scheve. 2007. "Estimating the Effect of Elite Communications on Public Opinion Using Instrumental Variables." *American Journal of Political Science* 51 (4): 1013–1028.

Gamble, Katrina. 2007. "Black Political Representation: An Examination of Legislative Activity Within U.S. House Committees." *Legislative Studies Quarterly* 32 (3): 421–447.

Gerber, Alan, and Neil Malhotra. 2008. "Do Statistical Reporting Standards Affect What is Published? Publication Bias in Two Leading Political Science Journals." *Quarterly Journal of Political Science* 3 (3): 313–326.

Gerber, Alan S., Donald P. Green, and David Nickerson. 2001. "Testing for Publication Bias in Political Science." *Political Analysis* 9 (4): 385–392.

Gerber, Alan S., Gregory A. Huber, David Doherty, and Conor M. Dowling. 2011. "Citizens' Policy Confidence and Electoral Punishment: A Neglected Dimension of Electoral Accountability." *Journal of Politics* 73 (4): 1206–1224.

Gerrity, Jessica C., Tracy Osborn, and Jeanette Morehouse Mendez. 2007. "Women and Representation: A Different View of the District." *Politics & Gender* 3 (2): 179–200.

Gertzog, Irwin. 1995. *Congressional Women: Their Recruitment, Integration, and Behavior*, 2nd ed. Westport, CT: Praeger Publishers.

Gilens, Martin. 2005. "Inequality and Democratic Responsiveness." *Public Opinion Quarterly* 69 (5): 778–796.

———. 2009. "Preference Gaps and Inequality in Representation." *PS: Political Science and Politics* 42(2): 335–341.

———. 2012. *Affluence and Influence: Economic Inequality and Political Power in America*. Princeton, NJ: Princeton University Press.

Gilligan, Thomas W., and Keith Krehbiel. 1989. "Asymmetric Information and Legislative Rules with a Heterogeneous Committee." *American Journal of Political Science* 33 (2): 459–490.

———. 1990. "Organization of Informative Committees by a Rational Legislature." *American Journal of Political Science* 34 (2): 531–564.

Goldschmidt, Kathy, and Leslie Ochreiter. 2008. *Communicating with Congress: How the Internet has Changed Citizen Engagement*. Washington, DC: Congressional Management Foundation.

Gramlich, Edward M., and Deborah S. Laren. 1984. "Migration and Income Distribution Responsibilities." *Journal of Human Resources* 19 (4): 489–511.

Grey, Sandra. 2006. "Numbers and Beyond: The Relevance of Critical Mass in Gender Research." *Politics & Gender* 2 (4): 492–502.

134 References

Griffin, John D., and Michael Keane. 2006. "Descriptive Representation and the Composition of African American Turnout." *American Journal of Political Science* 50 (4): 998–1012.

Griffin, John D. and Brian M. Newman. 2007. "The Unequal Representation of Latinos and Whites." *Journal of Politics* 69 (4): 1032–1046.

———. 2008. *Minority Report: Evaluating Political Equality in America.* Chicago: University of Chicago Press.

Griffin, John D., Brian Newman, and Christina Wolbrecht. 2012. "A Gender Gap in Policy Representation in the U.S. Congress?" *Legislative Studies Quarterly* 37 (1): 35–66.

Grose, Christian R. 2011. *Congress in Black and White: Race and Representation in Washington and at Home.* New York: Cambridge University Press.

Grose, Christian R., Maruice Mangum, and Christopher Martin. 2007. "Race, Political Empowerment, and Constituency Service: Descriptive Representation and the Hiring of African-American Congressional Staff." *Polity* 39 (4): 449–478.

Guinier, Lani. 1994. *The Tyranny of the Majority: Fundamental Fairness in Representative Democracy.* New York: Free Press.

Hajnal, Zoltan L. 2009. "Who Loses in American Democracy? A Count of Votes Demonstrates the Limited Representation of African Americans." *American Political Science Review* 103 (1): 35–57.

Hall, Richard L. 1996. *Participation in Congress.* New Haven, CT: Yale University Press.

Hall, Richard L., and Alan V. Deardorff. 2006. "Lobbying as Legislative Subsidy." *American Political Science Review* 100 (1): 69–84.

Hamburger, Tom, and Peter Wallsten. 2005. "Parties Are Tracking Your Habits. Though Both Democrats and Republicans Collect Personal Information, the GOP's Mastery of Data Is Changing the Very Nature of Campaigning." *Los Angeles Times*, July 25, p. 1.

Harden, Jeffrey J. 2013. "Multidimensional Democracy: The Determinants of Legislators' Representational Priorities." *Legislative Studies Quarterly* 38 (2): 155–184.

Haynie, Kerry. 2001. *African American Legislators in the American States.* New York: Columbia University Press.

Heath, Roseanna Michelle, Leslie A. Schwindt-Bayer, and Michelle M. Taylor-Robinson. 2005. "Women on the Sidelines: Women's Representation on Committees in Latin American Legislatures." *American Journal of Political Science* 49 (2): 420–436.

Heckman, James J. 1998. "Detecting Discrimination." *Journal of Economic Perspectives* 12 (2): 101–116.

Heckman, James J. and Peter Siegelman. 1992. "The Urban Institute Audit Studies: Their Methods and Findings." in Michael Fix and Raymond J. Struyk, eds. *Clear and Convincing Evidence: Measurement of Discrimination in America.* Lanham, MD: Urban Institute Press.

Hernandez, Raymond. 2006. "After Challenges, House Approves Renewal of Voting Act." *New York Times*, July 14.

Hero, Rodney E., and Caroline J. Tolbert. 1995. "Latinos and Substantive Representation in the U.S. House of Representatives: Direct, Indirect, or Nonexistent?" *American Journal of Political Science* 39 (3): 640–652.

Hillygus, S. Sunshine, and Todd G. Shields. 2008. *The Persuadable Voter: Wedge Issues in Presidential Campaigns.* Princeton, NJ: Princeton University Press.

Hoffman, L. Richard, and Norman R. F. Maier. 1961. "Quality and acceptance of problem solutions by members of homogenous and heterogeneous groups." *Journal of Abnormal and Social Psychology* 62 (2): 401–407.

Hood, M.V. III, and Irvin L. Morris. 1998. "Boll Weevils and Roll-Call Voting: A Study in Time and Space." *Legislative Studies Quarterly* 23 (2): 245–69.

Hutchings, Vincent. 1998. "Issue Salience and Support for Civil Rights Legislation among Southern Democrats." *Legislative Studies Quarterly* 23 (4): 521–544.

Hutchings, Vincent L., and Nicholas A. Valentino. 2004. "The Centrality of Race in American Politics." *Annual Review of Political Science* 7: 383–408.

Imbens, Guido W., and Thomas Lemieux. 2008. "Regression Discontinuity Designs: A Guide to Practice." *Journal of Econometrics* 142 (2): 615–635.

Iyengar, Shanto, and Joel B. Greenhouse. 1988. "Selection Models and the File Drawer Problem." *Statistical Science* 3 (1): 109–117.

Iyengar, Shanto, Kyu S. Hahn, Jon A. Krosnick, and John Walker. 2008. Selective Exposure to Campaign Communication: The Role of Anticipated Agreement and Issue Public Membership." *Journal of Politics* 70 (1): 186–200.

Jacobs, Lawrence R., and Benjamin I. Page. 2005. "Who Influences U.S. Foreign Policy?" *American Political Science Review* 99 (1): 107–123.

Jacobs, Lawrence R., and Robert Y. Shapiro. 2000. *Politicians Don't Pander: Political Manipulation and the Loss of Democratic Responsiveness.* Chicago: University Of Chicago Press.

———. 2005. "Polling Politics, Media, and Election Campaigns." *Public Opinion Quarterly* 69 (5): 635–641.

Jacobs, Lawrence R., Eric D. Lawrence, Robert Y. Shapiro, and Steven S. Smith. 1998. "Congressional Leadership of Public Opinion." *Political Science Quarterly* 113 (1): 21–41.

Kanter, Rosabeth Moss. 1977. "Some Effects of Proportions on Group Life: Skewed Sex Ratios and Responses to Token Women." *American Journal of Sociology* 82 (5): 965–990.

Kellman, Laurie. 2006. "House Renews Voting Rights Act Unchanged." *Associated Press*, July 14.

Kerr, Brinck, and Will Miller. 1997. "Latino Representation, It's Direct and Indirect." *American Journal of Political Science* 41 (3): 1066–1071.

King, Gary. 1991. "Constituency Service and Incumbency Advantage." *British Journal of Political Science* 21 (1): 119–128.

Kingdon, John W. 1981. *Congressmen's Voting Decisions*, 2nd ed. New York: Harper & Row.

Krehbiel, Keith. 1991. *Information and Legislative Organization.* Ann Arbor, MI: University of Michigan Press.

Krosnick, Jon A. 1990. "Americans' Perceptions of Presidential Candidates: A Test of the Projection Hypothesis." *Journal of Social Issues* 46 (2): 159–182.

Lauderdale, Benjamin E., 2010. Does Congress Represent Public Opinion as it is or as it Might Be? APSA 2010 Annual Meeting Paper. Available at SSRN: http://ssrn.com/abstract=1644632.

Lawless, Jennifer L. 2004. "Politics of Presence: Congresswomen in the House and Symbolic Representation." *Political Research Quarterly* 57 (1): 81–99.

Lee, David S. 2008. "Randomized Experiments from Non-Random Selection in U.S. House Elections." *Journal of Econometrics* 142 (2): 675–697.

Lijphart, Arend. 1997. "Unequal Participation: Democracy's Unresolved Dilemma." *American Political Science Review* 91 (1): 1–14.

Lodge, Milton, and Charles Taber. 2000. "Three Steps toward a Theory of Motivated Political Reasoning." In *Elements of Reason: Cognition, Choice, and the Bounds of Rationality*, eds. Arthur Lupia, Mathew McCubbins, and Samuel Popkin. London: Cambridge University Press.

Lublin, David I. 1997. *The Paradox of Representation: Racial Gerrymandering and Minority Interests in Congress*. Princeton, NJ: Princeton University Press.

Mahoney, Michael J. 1977. "Publication Prejudices: An Experimental Study of Confirmatory Bias in the Peer Review System." *Cognitive Therapy and Research* 1 (2): 161–175.

Manley, John F. 1983. "Neo-Pluralism: A Class Analysis of Pluralism I and Pluralism II." *American Political Science Review* 77 (2): 368–383.

Mansbridge, Jane. 1999. "Should Blacks Represent Blacks and Women Represent Women? A Contingent 'Yes.'" *Journal of Politics* 61 (3): 628–657.

Marley, Patrick, Bill Glauber, and Steve Schultze. 2011. "Caller Posing as Major GOP Contributor Dupes Walker." *Milwaukee Journal Sentinel*, February 23.

Mayhew, David R. 2008. "Incumbency Advantage in U.S. Presidential Elections: The Historical Record." *Political Science Quarterly* 123 (2): 201–228.

McConnell, Sheena, Elizabeth A. Stuart, and Barbara Devaney. 2008. "The Truncation-by-Death Problem: What to do in an Experimental Evaluation When the Outcome is Not Always Defined." *Evaluation Review* 32 (2): 157–186.

McDermott, Rose. 2002. "Experimental Methods in Political Science." *Annual Review of Political Science* 5: 31–61.

———. 2013. "The Ten Commandments of Experiments." *PS: Political Science & Politics* 46 (3): 605–610.

McPherson, Miller, Lynn Smith-Lovin, and James M. Cook. 2001. "Birds of a Feather: Homophily in Social Networks." *Annual Review of Sociology* 27: 415–444.

Mendelberg, Tali. 2001. *The Race Card: Campaign Strategy, Implicit Messages, and the Norm of Equality*. Princeton, NJ: Princeton University Press.

Miler, Kristina C. 2007. "The View from the Hill: Legislative Perceptions of Constituents." *Legislative Studies Quarterly* 33 (4): 597–628.

———. 2010. *Constituency Representation in Congress: The View from Capitol Hill*. Cambridge: Cambridge University Press.

Minta, Michael D. 2009. "Legislative Oversight and the Substantive Representation of Black and Latino Interests in Congress." *Legislative Studies Quarterly* 34 (2): 193–218.

———. 2011. *Oversight: Representing the Interests of Blacks and Latinos in Congress*. Princeton, NJ: Princeton University Press.

National Conference of State Legislators. 2013. "Former State Legislators in Congress." http://www.ncsl.org/legislatures-elections/state-federal/former-state-legislators-in-congress.aspx. Accessed: July 17, 2013.

Norton, Noelle H., 1999. "Committee Influence over Controversial Policy: The Reproductive Policy Case." *Policy Studies Journal* 27 (2): 203–216.

Orey, Byron D'Andra, Wendy Smooth, Kimberly S. Adams, and Kisha Harris-Clark. 2006. "Race and Gender Matter: Rethinking Models of Legislative Policy making in State Legislatures." *Journal of Women, Politics & Policy* 28 (3/4): 97–119.

Ornstein, Norman J., and Thomas E. Mann, eds. 2000. *The Permanent Campaign and its Future*. Washington, D.C.: American Enterprise Institute; Brookings Institution.

Overby, L. Marvin, and Kenneth M. Cosgrove. 1996. "Unintended Consequences? Racial Redistricting and the Representation of Minority Interests." *Journal of Politics* 58: 540–550.

Pager, Devah. 2007. "The Use of Field Experiments for Studies of Employment Discrimination: Contributions, Critiques, and Directions for the Future." *Annals of the American Academy of Political and Social Science* 609 (1): 104–133.

Pager, Devah, and Lincoln Quillian. 2005. "Walking the Talk? What Employers Say Versus What They Do." *American Sociological Review* 70 (3): 355–380.

Pager, Devah, Bruce Western, and Bart Bonikowski. 2009. "Discrimination in a Low Wage Labor Market: A Field Experiment." *American Sociology Review* 74 (October): 777–799.

Palmer, Barbara, and Dennis Simon. 2006. *Breaking the Political Glass Ceiling: Women and Congressional Elections*. New York: Routledge.

Pande, Rohini. 2003. "Can Mandated Political Representation Increase Policy Influence from Disadvantaged Minorities? Theory and Evidence from India." *American Economic Review* 93 (4): 1132–1151.

Peterson, Paul E., and Mark C. Rom. 1989. "American Federalism, Welfare Policy and Residential Choices." *American Political Science Review* 83 (3): 711–728.

———. 1990. *Welfare Magnets: A New Case for a National Standard*. Washington, DC: Brookings Institution.

Pitkin, Hanna F. 1967. *The Concept of Representation*. Berkeley: University California Press.

Piven, Frances Fox and Richard A. Cloward. 1988. *Why Americans Don't Vote*. New York: Pantheon.

Poole, Keith T. 2007. "Changing Minds? Not in Congress!" *Public Choice* 131 (3/4): 435–451.

Putnam, Robert D. 1993. *Making Democracy Work: Civic Traditions in Modern Italy*. Princeton, NJ: Princeton University Press.

Putnam, Robert D., and David E. Campbell. 2010. *American Grace: How Religion Divides and Unites Us*. New York: Simon & Schuster.

Radcliff, Benjamin, and Martin Saiz. 1995. "Race, Turnout, and Public Policy in the American States." *Political Research Quarterly* 48 (4): 775–794.

Rainey, James. 2011. "On the Media: NPR Video Stings Ethics Too." *Los Angeles Times*, March 11.

Rasmusen, Eric. 1993. "Lobbying When the Decisionmaker Can Acquire Independent Information." *Public Choice* 77 (4): 899–913.

Redlawsk, David P. 2002. "Hot Cognition or Cool Consideration? Testing the Effects of Motivated Reasoning on Political Decision Making." *Journal of Politics* 64 (4): 1021–1044.

Reingold, Beth. 1992. Concepts of Representation Among Female and Male State Legislators." *Legislative Studies Quarterly* 17 (4): 509–537.

———. 2008. "Women as Office Holders: Linking Descriptive and Substantive Representation." In *Political Women and American Democracy: Critical Perspectives on*

Women and Politics Research, ed. Christina Wolbrecht, Karen Beckwith, and Lisa Baldez. New York: Cambridge University Press, 128–147.

Rigby, Elizabeth and Gerald Wright. 2011. "Whose Statehouse Democracy? Policy Responsiveness to Poor versus Rich Constituents in Poor versus Rich States." In *Who Gets Represented?*, ed. Peter Enns and Christopher Wlezien. New York: Russell Sage.

Rocca, Michael S., Gabriel R. Sanchez, and Joseph Uscinski. 2008. "Personal Attributes and Latino Voting Behavior in Congress." *Social Science Quarterly* 89 (2): 392–405.

Rosenstone, Steven J. and John Mark Hansen. 1993. *Mobilization, Participation, and Democracy in America*. New York: Macmillan.

Rothenberg, Lawrence S., and Mitchell S. Sanders. 2000. "Severing the Electoral Connection: Shirking in the Contemporary Congress." *American Journal of Political Science* 44 (2): 316–325.

Saint-Germain, Michelle A. 1989. "Does their Difference Make a Difference? The Impact of Women on Public Policy in the Arizona State Legislature." *Social Science Quarterly* 70 (4): 956–968.

Salisbury, Robert H., and Kenneth A. Shepsle. 1981a. "Congressional Staff Turnover and the Ties-That-Bind." *American Political Science Review* 75 (2): 381–396.

———. 1981b. "Congressman as Enterprise." *Legislative Studies Quarterly* 6 (4): 559–576.

Santos, Adolfo, and Carlos C. Huerta. 2001. "An Analysis of Descriptive and Substantive Latino Representation in Congress." In *Representation of Minority Groups in the U.S.: Implications for the Twenty-First Century*, ed. Charles E. Menifield. Lanham, Maryland: Austin and Winfield Publishers.

Schattschneider, E.E. 1960. *The Semisovereign People: A Realist's View of Democracy in America*. New York: Holt, Reinhart, and Winston.

Schiller, Wendy J. 2000. *Partners and Rivals: Representation in U.S. Senate Delegations*. Princeton, NJ: Princeton University Press.

Schlozman, Kay Lehman, Sidney Verba, and Henry E. Brady. 2012. *The Unheavenly Chorus: Unequal Political Voice and the Broken Promise of American Democracy*. Princeton, NJ: Princeton University Press.

Sears, David O. 1986. "College Sophomores in the Laboratory: Influences of a Narrow Data Base on Social Psychology's View of Human Nature." *Journal of Personality and Social Psychology* 51 (3): 515–530.

Serra, George and Albert D. Cover. 1992. "The Electoral Consequences of Perquisite Use: The Casework Case." *Legislative Studies Quarterly* 17 (2): 233–246.

Sinclair-Chapman, Valeria. 2002. *Symbols and Substance*. Ph.D. Dissertation. Ohio State University.

Sinclair-Chapman, Valeria, and Melanie Price. 2008. "Black Politics, the 2008 Election, and the (Im)Possibility of Race Transcendence." *PS: Political Science and Politics* 41 (October): 739–745.

Sniderman, Paul M., and Edward G. Carmines. 1997. *Reaching Beyond Race*. Cambridge, MA: Harvard University Press.

Snyder, James M., and Michiko Ueda. 2007. "Do Multimember Districts Lead to Free-Riding?" *Legislative Studies Quarterly* 32 (4): 649–679.

Squire, Peverill. 1992. "Legislative Professionalization and Membership Diversity in State Legislatures." *Legislative Studies Quarterly* 17 (1): 69–79.

———. 2007. "Measuring State Legislative Professionalism: The Squire Index Revisited." *State Politics and Policy Quarterly* 7 (2): 211–227.

Stimson, James A. 2009. "Perspectives on *Unequal Democracy: The Political Economy of the New Gilded Age.*" *Perspectives on Politics* 7 (1): 151–153.

Storing, Herbert J., ed. 1981. *The Complete Anti-Federalist.* 7 vols. Chicago, IL: University of Chicago Press.

Swain, Carol M. 1993. *Black Faces, Black Interests: The Representation of African Americans in Congress.* Cambridge, MA: Harvard University.

Swers, Michele L. 1998. "Are Women More Likely to Vote for Women's Issue Bills than their Male Colleagues?" *Legislative Studies Quarterly* 23 (3): 435–448.

_____. 2001. "Understanding the Policy Impact of Electing Women: Evidence from Research on Congress and State Legislatures." *PS: Political Science and Politics* 34 (2): 217–220.

_____. 2002. *The Difference Women Make: The Policy Impact of Women in Congress.* Chicago: University of Chicago Press.

Swers, Michele L. and Stella M. Rouse. 2011. "Descriptive Representation: Understanding the Impact of Identity on Substantive Representation of Group Interests." In *The Oxford Handbook of the American Congress,* ed. Eric Schickler and Frances E. Lee. New York: Oxford University Press.

Tamerius, Karin L. 1995. "Sex, Gender, and Leadership in the Representation of Women." In *Gender, Power, Leadership and Governance,* ed. Georgia Duerst-Lahti and Rita Mae Kelly. Ann Arbor: University of Michigan Press.

Tatalovitch, Raymond, and David Schier. 1993. "The Persistence of Ideological Cleavage in Voting on Abortion Legislation in the House of Representatives, 1973–1988." *American Politics Research* 21 (1): 125–139.

Tate, Katherine. 2003. *Black Faces in the Mirror: African Americans and their Representatives in Congress.* Princeton, NJ: Princeton University Press.

Tax Policy Center. 2013. "The Numbers: What is the breakdown of revenues among federal, state and local governments?" http://www.taxpolicycenter.org/briefing-book/background/numbers/revenue-breakdown.cfm. Accessed July 16, 2013.

Thomas, Sue. 1994. *How Women Legislate.* New York: Oxford University Press.

_____. 1997. "Why Gender Matters: The Perceptions of Women Officeholders." *Women & Politics* 17: 27–53.

Thomas, Sue, and Susan Welch. 1991. "The Impact of Gender on Activities and Priorities of State Legislators." *Western Political Quarterly* 44 (2): 445–456.

Thurber, Timothy N. 2004. "Second Reconstruction," in *The American Congress: The Building of Democracy,* ed. Julian E. Zelizer. Boston: Houghton-Mifflin Company: 529–547.

Trounstine, Jessica. 2009. "All Politics is Local." *Perspectives on Politics* 7 (3): 611–618.

Udall, Morris K. 1967. "The Right to Write: Some Suggestions on Writing Your Congressman." Congressman's Report Vol. 6, No. 1, January 20, 1967.

Ura, Joseph Daniel and Christopher R. Ellis. 2008. "Income, Preferences, and the Dynamics of Policy Responsiveness." *PS: Political Science and Politics* 41 (4): 785–794.

Van Knippenberg, Daan, Carsten K.W. De Dreu, Astrid C. Homan. 2004. "Work Group Diversity and Group Performance: An Integrative Model and Research Agenda." *Journal of Applied Psychology* 89 (6): 1008–1022.

Verba, Sidney. 2003. "Would the Dream of Political Equality Turn Out to Be a Nightmare?" *Perspectives on Politics* 1 (4): 663–679.

Verba, Sidney, and Norman H. Nie. 1972. *Participation in America: Political Democracy and Social Equality.* New York: Harper and Row.

Verba, Sidney, Kay Lehman Schlozman, and Henry E. Brady. 1995. *Voice and Equality: Civic Voluntarism in American Politics.* Cambridge, MA: Harvard University Press.

Wallace, Sophia J. 2010 "Beyond Roll Call Votes: Latino Representation in the 108–110th Sessions of the U.S. House of Representatives." Ph.D. Dissertation. Department of Government. Cornell University.

Wasniewski, Matthew, ed. 2008. *Black Americans in Congress, 1870–2007.* Washington, D.C.: U.S. Government Printing Office.

Weingast, Barry R. and William J. Marshall. 1988. "The Industrial Organization of Congress; or, Why Legislatures, Like Firms, Are Not Organized as Markets." *Journal of Political Economy* 96 (1): 132–163.

Welch, Susan, and John Hibbing. 1984. "Hispanic Representation in the U.S. Congress." *Social Science Quarterly* 65 (2): 328–335. Reprinted in *Latinos and the Political System*, ed. F. Chris Garcia. Notre Dame: University of Notre Dame Press.

Whitby, Kenny J. 1997. *The Color of Representation: Congressional Behavior and Black Interests.* Ann Arbor: University of Michigan Press.

Wlezien, Christopher. 2004. "Patterns of Representation: Dynamics of Public Preferences and Policy." *Journal of Politics* 66 (1):1–24.

Wlezien, Christopher and Stuart N. Soroka. 2011. "Inequality in Policy Responsiveness?" *Who Gets Represented?* Peter Enns and Christopher Wlezien, Eds. New York: Russell Sage.

Wolbrecht, Christina. 2002. "Female Legislators and the Women's Rights Agenda: From Feminine Mystique to Feminist Era." In *Women Transforming Congress*, ed. Cindy Simon Rosenthal. Norman: University of Oklahoma Press, 170–239.

Wolbrecht, Christina, and David E. Campbell. 2007. "Leading by Example: Female Members of Parliament as Political Role Models." *American Journal of Political Science* 51 (October): 921–939.

Word, David L., Charles D. Coleman, Robert Nunziata, and Robert Kominski. n.d. "Demographic Aspects of Surnames from Census 2000." *Technical Report for the U.S. Census Bureau.* http://www.census.gov/genealogy/www/surnames.pdf.

Index

Note: page numbers followed by *b, f, n,* or *t* indicate boxes, figures, notes, or tables respectively.

bias related to race and, 117n
elite, candidate emergence research and, 127
equal representation and equal treatment and, 117
by high-SES vs. low-SES individuals, 49
research on representation and inequality and, 127
types of and responses to, 31
politicians. *See also* Congress, members of; legislators; mayors
issue salience, issue information, and decision-making by, 18–19
poll results, public officials on constituents' understanding of issues and, 17–18
Pope, Jeremy C., 27–28, 36–37, 89–90
preclearance provision, Voting Rights Act, 113–114, 114f, 115
primary elections. *See also* elections
state legislators' responsiveness to constituents' requests and, 91–93
professionalism of legislative offices
diverse staffs and, 126
responses to constituency service field experiments and, 23–24, 24n
proportionality standard, representation and, 81
public library. *See* library, public
public opinion, constituents' political knowledge and, 44
public policies, race, ethnicity, party and, 112–113
public schools, personal roots of representation and choices with regard to using, 4n
Putnam, Robert D., 24, 26

questions
used in constituency service field experiments, 39–42
used in information and gender study, 76t, 77, 77n
used in personal bias and race and ethnicity study, 93, 95n
used in personal bias and race study, 86–87

racial and ethnic groups. *See also* blacks; Latinos
aliases used to indicate, 90t, 90
bias against, descriptive representation and, 10
bias in representation of, 120–121, 121t
Griffin and Newman on voter representation and, 3

legislative staff background and casework for, 7
legislators' perceptions of letters and, 45–46
legislators' race and responsiveness to, 30–31
measuring legislators' bias toward, 4–5
numbers in Congress vs. state and local officials, 26–27
partisanship, public policies and, 112–113
preferences of, as policy change predictors, 2–3
representatives' responsiveness and political participation by, 31
state legislators' bias in processing opinions by, 53–54, 54b, 55t, 56
strategic discrimination and information conveyed by, 20–21
testing for nonstrategic bias against, 19–20
racial discrimination
elections by plurality vote and, 119–120
federal agency audits of government programs on, 25n
gender discrimination compared to, 122–123
personal preferences of state legislators and, 86–87, 87b, 93–94, 94b, 96t, 96n, 96, 98
politician's personal preferences and, 118
racial redistricting
Democrats in office and, 115–116
in Georgia (1995), 16
maximizing political interests of minority voters and, 124–126
substantive representation and debates on, 99–100
rationalizations, for discounting some constituents' opinions, 17, 43–44, 44n, 45
Reagan, Ronald, 2
reelection-motivated politicians
elections by plurality vote and, 119–120
importance of information for, 62–63
inequality and, 127
information costs shaping behavior of, 13–14, 118
information differences as source of bias in, 5–6
responses to constituents' requests by, 35–37
voter targeting by, 19–20
religious affiliation
choices with regard to using public schools and, 4n
gender bias compared to discrimination due to, 122–123